THE WYE VALLEY WALK

*The
History and Heritage
People and Places
Flora and Fauna
of a Noble River*

Heather & Jon Hurley

Maps and drawings by
David Grech

Thornhill Press Ltd.
Publishers

―――――― **DEDICATION** ――――――

To walkers everywhere
and those who make it easy for them.

Published 1994 by Thornhill Press Ltd.
Parkend, Nr Lydney, Glos.
© Jon & Heather Hurley 1994

ISBN 0 946328 34 X
Typeset in Palatino 10pt by *Walkers' World*
Printed in England by Hillman Printers (Frome) Ltd, Frome, Somerset.

❖ CONTENTS ❖

———————————— *The* ————————————

Wye Valley Walk

is jointly managed as a regional recreational route by
Gwent, Hereford & Worcester and *Powys*
County Councils.

The Authors

Heather and Jon Hurley live with their children in the heart of the Wye Valley from where, for the past twenty years, they have run their now nationally known, **WineWeekends**.

Between them they have accumulated a considerable knowledge of the Wye Valley and Welsh Borders by walking it thoroughly, and researching for their books. Their previous publications include *"Paths and Pubs of the Wye Valley"* and *"Rambles and Refreshments on the Welsh Borders"*, published by **Thornhill Press Ltd**.

Heather, a keen local historian, a Countryside Warden and Chair of the Ross Civic Society's Rights-of-Way Committee, has first hand experience of conservation, keeping footpaths open, and leading walks.

Jon lectures, writes and broadcasts on wine and plays golf, travels to the great vineyards, and, like Heather, enjoys gardening and countryside activities.

Acknowledgements

The authors wish to record their appreciation for the kind assistance, support and co-operation gratefully received from:
Chepstow Library, Museum and Tourist Information Centre; The Old Station, Tintern; Monmouth Library, Museum and Tourist Information Centre; Ross-on-Wye Library and Tourist Information Centre; Hereford Library, Museum, Record Office and Tourist Information Centre; Hay-on-Wye Tourist Information Centre; Builth Wells Library and Tourist Information Centre, Rhayader Museum and Tourist Information Centre; Elan Valley Visitor Centre; the Forestry Commission; National Rivers Authority; Radnorshire Wildlife Trust; Gwent Countryside Service; Hereford and Worcester Countryside Service; Powys County Council.

We also wish to thank Rosemary Jones for typing; and all our friends who walked part of the way with us, especially Sharon Clayton who looked after Alice our daughter.

Grey Heron.

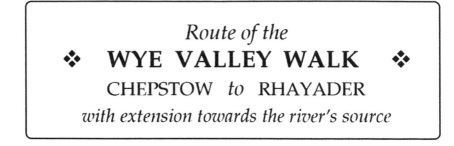

Route of the
❖ WYE VALLEY WALK ❖
CHEPSTOW *to* RHAYADER
with extension towards the river's source

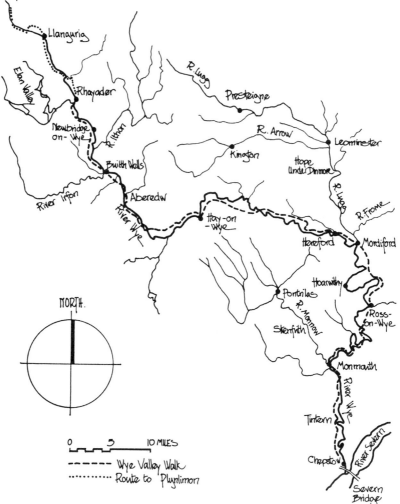

6

❖ *Introduction* ❖

The Wye Valley Walk's often shy beauty richly deserves the admiration of discerning walkers. Searching the river from tidal banks, via an English vale and verdant winding valleys, it ventures towards the river's source, at the very heart of upland Wales. In essence it is a walk ideally suited to the casual family walker.

This waymarked trail, is lapped by the River Wye, one of Britain's great rivers, offering the walker a journey through gentle, undulating countryside, with lofty views of secluded farms and silent forests, gentle ascents, woodland paths bedecked with wild flowers where silence is punctuated only by bird-song and one's own footfall.

Throughout its length are signs of man's impact on and intrusion into the landscape, there are Iron Age hill-forts, abandoned mines and watermills, ruined castles and monasteries, tiny churches that fit so snugly into the landscape they could have grown there, and solid stone and timber farmsteads that have stubbornly resisted the passing of time. There is evidence of more recent immigration the refurbished, rose cuddled cottages with manicured lawns and once derelict barns snatched from oblivion by those seeking a lovely place in which to retire.

For the nature lover the Wye Valley Walk is one meandering, ever changing reserve. Trees abound, with great oaks, beech, ash, alder trailing its branches in the river as well as ubiquitous softwood bedecking every bald hill. Wild flowers galore adorn river banks, catching the sun in spring and summer and secreted in dark places in winter, whilst a wide array of colourful fungi, often edible, sprout and climb. It is a haven for many spieces of bird that can be observed and enjoyed as they sing, flock, swirl, swoop, croak and call. Among the animals that frequent the area is the wily fox, the secretive and endangered otter and his ravenous neighbour, the voracious mink, deer shyly hiding in woodland and the badger in ever increasing numbers.

Fields, often framed by trees, offer stunning views of distant hills reflecting the valley's main industry, farming. Alongside stone cider houses are orchards, delightful in spring with their smudged pink and white blossom and tempting in autumn with boughs hanging low with rouged fruit, please note that cider apples are not eating apples: a few intrepid cider makers still practise their ancient art. Hops festoon the hedgerows, a reminder of the days when ale brewing was a cottage industry.

The mature River Wye is renowned for offering excellent angling from the slippery eel, lurking under the rocks, to the fine salmon, alas now in dwindling numbers, leaping upstream to spawn.

The book guides the more ambitious walker to this great river's humble beginnings, a mere trickle of deliciously fresh spring water oozing from a crack in the ground high up on Plynlimon in 'remote' mid-Wales. To walk beside the river all the way to its source demands commitment, a small price to pay for so much pleasure. It is a richly rewarding experience, offering a unique insight into the people, places, history and wildlife of the beautiful Wye Valley.

Waymarking and Path Management

As presently designated, the Wye Valley Walk runs from Chepstow to Rhayader, a distance of some 125 miles. The route is clearly distinguished by the leaping Salmon waymark (right), from time to time there may be changes, so if in doubt, follow the Salmon logo waymarks.

Heather and Jon have carefully plotted and described a practical route for the remaining 25 miles towards the river's source. This section is not part of the officially waymarked Wye Valley Walk and is entirely the work of the authors.

If any difficulties are encountered, or further information is required on any section of the route, please contact the relevant County Council Authority :

CHEPSTOW to THE BIBLINS
Planning & Economic Development Department,
Gwent County Council,
CWMBRAN, Gwent NP44 2XF

THE BIBLINS to HAY-ON-WYE
The Countryside Service,
Queenswood Country Park, Dinmore Hill,
LEOMINSTER, Hereford & Worcester HR6 0PY

HAY-ON-WYE to RHAYADER
(and the rights-of-way between Rhayader and Plynlimon)
Rights of Way & Countryside Section,
Planning Department, Powys County Council,
County Hall, LLANDRINDOD WELLS,
Powys LD1 5LG

Chapter 1

CHEPSTOW *to* MONMOUTH

— FACT FILE —

Distance
20 miles (32.5 km)

Map
O.S.Landranger sheet 162

Transport
The Lower Wye Valley is served by trains to Chepstow with buses running between Chepstow and Monmouth. For details contact British Rail or telephone Chepstow ☎ *622947 for bus times.*

Parking
Chepstow Castle, Lower Wyndcliff, Tintern Abbey, the Old Station Tintern, Whitestone, Manor Wood and Monmouth.

Picnic sites
Lower Wyndcliff, the Old Station Tintern and Whitestone.

Refreshments
Chepstow, Tintern, Brockweir, The Narth, Redbrook and Monmouth.

Accommodation and general visitor information
Tourist Information Centres at :
Chepstow ☎ *02912 3772,*
Monmouth ☎ *0600 713899*
Coleford ☎ *0594 836307.*

Camp Sites
Located at Chepstow, Brockweir, Llandogo, Whitebrook and Monmouth.
☎ *the nearest TIC for details.*

Youth Hostels
St Briavels and Monmouth.
Contact the Youth Hostels Association ☎ *0727 855215.*

Circular Walks
There are a selection of waymarked routes including those from Lower Wyndcliff, Tintern Abbey, Old Station Tintern, Whitestone, Manor Wood and The Kymin. For further information contact Gwent County Council ☎ *0633 832787 or the nearest Tourist Information Centre.*

Gwent Countryside Service *Wye Valley AONB office, Hadnock Rd, Mayhill, Monmouth* ☎ *0600 713977.*

Public Telephones
Chepstow, Tintern, Cleddon, Pen-y-fan, The Narth, Whitebrook, Penalt and Monmouth.

Public Toilets
Chepstow, Tintern, Whitestone (seasonal) and Monmouth.

☞ ROUTE DIRECTIONS ☜

The **Wye Valley Walk** is a waymarked route. Follow distinctive Salmon signs directing along a tarmac lane, beneath the castle's massive walls to **Castle Dell**. Continue along a short stretch of main road to **Chepstow Leisure Centre**. Cross the stile beyond the display board, to get your first glorious sensation of this superb long distance walk.

Now in attractive woodland, the path follows the **Piercefield Walks** twisting and turning between ancient yew, mature beech and yellowing lime, along a steep precipice high above the glistening **River Wye**. This course, laid out by Valentine Morris in 18th century, was known for its viewpoints: their remains may still be identified under cloaks of ivy.

The route tunnels its way through the **Giant's Cave** passing a place previously called the **Cold Bath**, then crosses a shallow brook. A series of wooden steps, built by the Wye Valley Wardens, eases a steep ascent to the **Wyndcliff** car park with its **Forest Nature Reserve**, picnic site and pleasing tree-framed view of the river.

Cross the main **Chepstow/Monmouth** road, turning sharply left at a quarry, a track climbs to the **Upper Wyncliff** but the path bears right, passing seats and viewpoints, including the **Eagle's Nest**. 700 feet above the **Wye**, this scenic lookout, offers spectacular views of the river's horseshoe bend around the **Lancaut** with the stone cliffs of **Wintour's Leap** beyond and the **Severn Suspension Bridge** in the distance.

A narrow path meanders from the **Eagle's Nest** through beech wood passing redundant pits and quarries. The **Wye** appears again below the **Black Cliff**: take great care do not stray near the sheer cliff face. Descend the remains of an early settlement, now an overgrown earthwork, the incline is steep and slippery.

A well signed path leads over a stile out of the woods. Yellow arrows direct the way across a field to another stile leading into

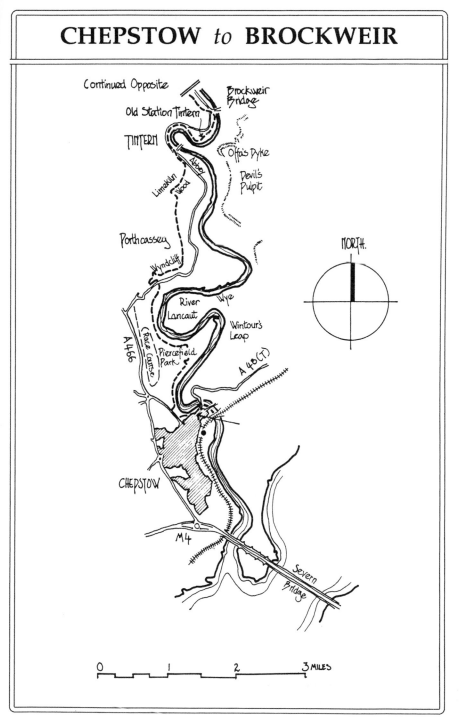

BROCKWEIR *to* MONMOUTH

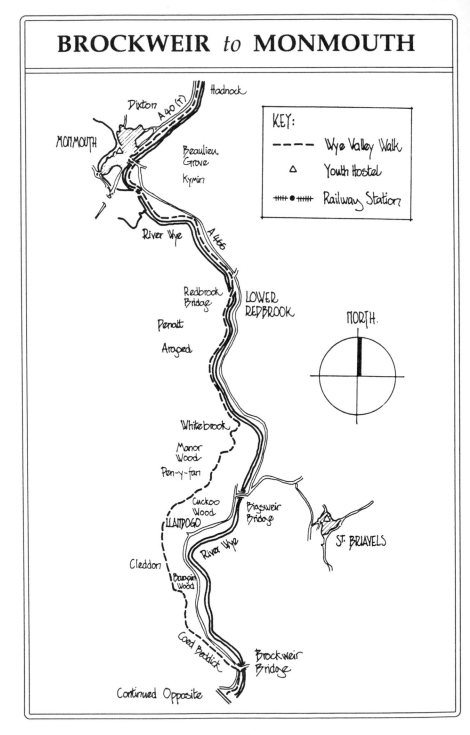

KEY:

- - - - Wye Valley Walk

△ Youth Hostel

┼┼┼•┼┼┼ Railway Station

NORTH.

Hadnock

Dixton
A 40 (T)

MONMOUTH

Beaulieu
Grove

Kymin

River Wye

A 466

Redbrook
Bridge

LOWER
REDBROOK

Penalt

Arayed

Whitebrook

Manor
Wood

Pen-y-fan

Cuckoo
Wood

LLANDOGO

Bigsweir
Bridge

ST. BRIAVELS

Cleddon

River Wye

Bargain
Wood

Coed Beddick

Brockweir
Bridge

Continued Opposite

Limekiln Wood. Descend to a former pack-horse road, and turn right following the old road to **Tintern** with a chattering brook for company.

The ruins of **Tintern Abbey** may be glimpsed before reaching a tarmac lane leading to the main road. Follow the road for about ½ mile through **Tintern** with its pubs, tea rooms and craft shops. Opposite the **Wye Valley Hotel**, bear right along a narrow lane leading into **St Michael's** churchyard, follow the delightful riverside path accompanying the Wye to a defunct railway embankment. Ascend the flight of concrete steps leading to the disused track and **Old Station**, now a visitor centre and popular tourist attraction, keep on the track to **Brockweir Bridge**. Turn left, cross the main road and take a narrow, signed, path that winds up a steep slope of bracken and shrubs. From a stone shed arrows mark a quiet route through the beech and conifer plantations of **Coed Beddick Wood**, gradually descend to **Botany Bay**.

Follow the minor road around a modern dwelling, immediately bearing right along a forest path leading to an unfenced tarmac lane. Walk left, then turn right following the waymarked route through **Bargain Wood** to the Forestry Commission's picnic site at **Whitestone**, from the forest track there is a series of magnificent views of the Wye and the village of **Llandogo**. Join the bridle-way and follow it to **Cleddon Shoots** where water tumbles and splashes down a steep ravine over moss covered boulders. A leaf-strewn track leads through **Cuckoo Wood** from the top of the falls, between the trees are some most attractive views.

The waymarked route directs via a gate, along an unfenced path to a further gate, a tarmac lane passes **Moor Cottage** and the entrance to **Woodfield House** at Pen-y-fan. Shortl after, bear left down a sunken way leading to pleasant green, with a time-worn mounting block and an inviting bench. Follow the lane past a renovated house called **The Green**, then in front of **Folly House** turn sharp right down the steep path to the **Whitebrook Valley**. Go right along the road through **Whitebrook** with its ruined mills and working farms.

Beyond **Tump Farm** turn left onto the old **Wye Valley Railway** track, walk along its course for about 2 miles between the slopes of **Hael Wood** and the banks of the gliding Wye. Before reaching a gate across the track, turn right over a stile, and follow the riverside through meadows to **Redbrook Bridge**. Walk under the bridge, bear left past the **Boat Inn** at Penallt, crossing the river via the iron bridge. From **Lower Redbrook** follow the waymarked route left, keeping close to the Wye until a stile leads to the road.

Follow the road leading away from the village for about 300 yards before returning to the riverside. This is a pleasant stretch through fields and a small wood: N.B. the narrow path close to the water's edge can be slippery after rain.

A stile leads out of the wood into meadows where the lofty **Kymin** overlooks ribbon development at **Wyesham** and the outskirts of **Monmouth**. The path narrows again as it follows the **Wye** below the picturesque remains of the **Wye Valley Railway** viaduct and the disused, rusting, metal **Ross to Monmouth** line bridge. From here the route skirts sports fields before reaching the **Wye Bridge** at **Monmouth**.

◆ HISTORIC WYE ◆

The Wye Valley Walk closely follows the banks of the river from Chepstow to Monmouth, a distance of twenty miles. The delightful route either hugs the meandering riverside or zig-zags steeply up wooded slopes with panoramic views of the Wye through the trees. Historic sites abound; prehistoric earthworks, Norman castles, interesting churches, the ruins of a Cistercian abbey, remains of picturesque walks and remnants of former railways, mills and furnaces. An abundance of political, artistic and literary characters including Turner, Wordsworth, Nelson, Russell and Shaw are associated with places in this area.

13th Century Town Arch at Chepstow.

Separated from England by the tidal River Wye, the small Welsh town of Chepstow developed over the centuries into an important market town and riverside port. The waters of Wye and Severn churn into white froth as they mingle uneasily below the gaunt suspension bridge, before entering the Bristol Channel. Starting from the castle

14

Chepstow's most striking and notable feature, the Wye Valley Walk has a most impressive send off on its long scenic journey to the source of the river in the remote hills of Plynlimon.

The towering remains of Chepstow's Norman Castle are the town's most striking and notable feature. The 11th century castle was built by William Fitz Osbern, created Earl of Hereford after the Conquest: Osbern's great tower still stands. Later additions increased the castle to its present size before the Civil War, the walls were breached when the Royalists surrendered to the Roundheads. During the Restoration the castle was used as a prison: the regicide Henry Marten spent twenty years of comfortable captivity in the tower now known as Marten's Tower. From the 17th century the building began to fall into decay; fortunately Chepstow Castle is now under the care of Welsh Historic Monuments, which provides visitors with an informative guidebook.

From Castle Dell a 13th century portwall extends around the town, which offered protection to Chepstow's once busy port. Wharves, timberyards and warehouses formerly lined the banks of the Wye, where warships, frigates, sloops and victualling vessels were built by Chepstow's skilled shipbuilders until the First World War. With easy access to Bristol, South Wales and Ireland it became a trading centre for wine, salt, fish, bark and timber.

From the 12th to the 19th century wine played an important part in the economy of the town. It began when Henry Plantagenet married Eleanor of Aquitaine in 1152, with his consent shippers of claret, a light red wine from Bordeaux, enjoyed a virtual monopoly of the English wine trade. There are constant references to Chepstow as a thriving wine town partly because its port held special custom privileges. Evidence of the part vintners played in the day to day workings of the town, and their conscientious and liberal attitudes, is expressed in the attractive almshouses built by Thomas Powis in 1721, a Middlesex wine merchant, who returned to Chepstow, his place of birth. Further evidence can be found in the tombs in the parish church, commemorating other wine merchants and vintners.

Oak bark, used in the process of tanning was exported in large quantities from Chepstow. The bark was collected by barges from forests at Monmouth, Redbrook, Llandogo, Brockweir and Tintern and conveyed to Chepstow for transportation to Bristol and Ireland. Some was retained for the town's own tanners who converted raw hides into leather for local craftsmen to make saddles, harness, shoes and gloves. The timber and bark trade reached its peak during the Napoleonic Wars, in 1799 over 9,000 tons of oak bark were exported from Chepstow.

Four strikingly different bridges cross the Wye at Chepstow.

Near the old port the Roman bridge was replaced by successive of structures over the centuries culminating in the present one built in 1816. Although attributed to Rennie, this fine cast-iron edifice was actually designed by John Rastrick, eventually unable to withstand heavy traffic it was abandoned and in 1988 a new bridge was constructed alongside Brunel's tubular railway bridge of 1852, which still carries a line from Gloucester to Cardiff. The last and most dramatic crossing is the Severn suspension bridge, which spans the Wye at its mouth, built in the late 1960s to link South Wales with the then new motorway system in England.

A short distance from the castle lies St Mary's parish church, altered and restored during the 19th century. It retains a spacious nave from its days as a Benedictine priory founded by Fitz Osbern. The squat tower, completed in 1706, stands above the west door, a fine example of Norman craftsmanship.

Amongst an array of fascinating tombs and monuments are a pre-Civil War organ, two fonts and the workings of an 18th century clock. The story of Henry Marten and his tomb, including an explanation of his clever epitaph can be found in St Mary's entrance. Today Chepstow offers both visitor and resident alike a neat and well ordered town, with excellent communications by road and rail. It is pleasantly situated beside the River Wye retaining an old fashioned charm with a cobbled street, arched town gate, almshouses and numerous buildings dating from the 18th and 19th centuries. Chepstow Museum traces the town's history through a series of displays depicting former trades, industries, crafts and early tourism, which began with the 18th century popular Wye Tour. Today shops, inns and tea-rooms offer an attractive range of goods and services. The small library houses some local material, but has become rather isolated since the re-routing of the busy A48. From May to September the Tourist Information Centre provides lists of accommodation and sites worth a visit.

The Wye Valley Walk leaves Chepstow and enters Pierce Woods with its sheer cliffs, dramatic vistas and scant remains of an 18th century Picturesque Walk laid out by Morris. Born in 1727, Valentine Morris inherited his father's estates in the West Indies and at Piercefield. During his sojourn in Monmouthshire he introduced new methods of agriculture, served as a turnpike trustee, and promoted a standard of weights and measures. By 1772 having squandered his fortune he returned to the West Indies, where he became Lieutenant Governor of St Vincent. He incurred further debts while defending the island during the American Civil War so was committed to the King's Bench Prison to be released, after the sale of Piercefield to George Smith, Morris spending his last days in London, where he died in 1789.

Gaunt overgrown ruins are all that remain of Smith's re-building of Piercefield House. His was a grand and ambitious design, a three storied mansion with stables, walled garden, greenhouse and grapery. The enterprise failed when Smith was de-clared bankrupt, the property passing to Lt. Colonel Wood, M.P., whose imaginative alterations almost constituted a new building. The crumbling outline of a Doric portico and ornamental wings of 1798 remain as a poignant reminder of man's frailty. In 1801 the house was purchased by Nathaniel Wells who fathered twenty children! After his death in 1852 until 1921, when it was sold to the Chepstow Racecourse Company, Piercefield frequently changed hands. The racetrack opened in 1926, and the once fine 'gentleman's residence' has been allowed to deteriorate to its present lamentable state of decay.

A leafy path winding through Pierce Wood is one of the high-lights of this section of the Wye Valley Walk. Although little remains of the 18th century Piercefield Walks, outstanding views can be enjoyed of Chepstow's great castle, the distant Severn, and the Wye flowing around the Lancaut peninsula below a backdrop of ragged cliffs. It is possible to identify remains of Valentine Morris' viewpoints, his Alcove, Platform, Grotto, Giant's Cave and Cold Bath. An alternative route to the Wyndcliff follows an undefined path from the Giant's Cave to Lover's Leap and the site of the Temple, demolished for the construction of the turnpike road in 1828, thus separating the Walks from the last spectacular prospect at the Wyndcliff.

From the Lower Wyndcliff picnic site a gradual climb leads walkers to the Eagles Nest, a Victorian lookout, over the counties of Gwent, Gloucestershire, Herefordshire, Avon, Somerset, Wiltshire and Powys. The stone seat commemorates a Wye Valley Warden involved with the initial planning and con-struction of the Wye Valley Walk.

Rising to over 700 feet these limestone crags offer an amazing panorama of one of the Wye's great horseshoe bends, encircling the Lancaut below the sheer cliffs of Wintour's Leap. These cliffs were named after Sir John Wintour, a Royalist from the Forest of Dean, who escaped Parliamentary pursuit during the Civil War by riding his horse down the cliff and across the Wye to safety - hence Wintour's Leap. The Eagles Nest can be reached via 365 steps twisting and turning up a gully between moss-covered boulders, past gaping caves and under ivy clad trees. The steps constructed in 1828 by the Duke of Beaufort's steward, were an added attraction

17

for the 19th century poets, writers and artists who visited the Wye Valley. The stone steps, renovated in 1971 by army apprentices, are now maintained by the Countryside Service. Moss Cottage, a rustic building which provided early Wye Tourists with refreshments and rest, once stood at the bottom .

In 1959 the Wyndcliff woods were established as a nature reserve with clematis, black bryony, and spindle growing along the waymarked path; maple, lime, wych elm, ash, oak, hazel and yew are also in evidence. Goldcrest, woodpeckers, wrens and finches are joined on sunny days by a variety of butterflies, including blues and fritillaries are attracted by the wild herbs and brambles. In autumn the woods smell of damp, decaying vegetation and fungi with names like Witches Butter, Tripe, Jew's Ear and Stickhorn abound: they come and go with surprising speed noted only by the expert delighting in their shapes, sizes and colour.

Before reaching Tintern the Wye Valley Walk joins an ancient packhorse road from Porthcasseg, with overhanging trees, deep rooted ferns and uneven rocky surface. It was the original route from Chepstow to Monmouth, superceded with the completion of the Turnpike in 1828. This thoroughfare extended along the river valley to Redbrook where it joined a route to Monmouth, turnpiked in 1755. 18th and 19th century road improvements opened up a hitherto isolated area previously served only by a maze of steep, narrow lanes or the navigable River Wye.

Tintern is famous for its magnificent ruins of the 12th century Cistercian abbey founded by Walter Fitz Richard de Clare from Chepstow. The monks became wealthy landowners and the abbey buildings were extended during their more prosperous years. At the time of the Dissolution the roofs and windows were vandalised leaving the abbey derelict.

In 1756 a forward thinking man from Chepstow employed a hundred men to clear the abbey site of tumbling masonry and debris. As a result artists, poets, writers and tourists were attracted to the ivy clad ruins at Tintern during the Romanic period of the 18th century. It has remained as a popular tourist feature attracting thousands of visitors every year to explore what has survived of its cloisters, dormitory, nave, choir and chapter house. The building is now under the protection of Welsh Historic Monuments which provides an excellent guidebook. During the Romantic period two notable characters visited the Wye Valley. The Hon. John Byng and the artist William Turner, who between them left written and visual accounts of Tintern at that time. John Byng, 5th Viscount of Torrington came from an illustrious naval background. He served as a soldier and civil servant and made a tour of England and Wales between 1781 and 1794. His journeys were described in the Torrington Diaries, which provide a colourful and valuable record of Tintern, Monmouth and Chepstow during the late 18th century.

Also at this time the young Joseph Mallord William Turner made a sketching tour of South Wales after studying at the Royal Academy in 1789. His works include water colours and prints of Tintern which survive in public and private collections. A coloured drawing of Hereford Cathedral was purchased by the Hereford Art Gallery in 1932 and still remains in their possession alongside other examples of his work.

With the decline of monastic life, Tintern thrived as a industrial site, recent archeological excavations indicate that smelting took place here before the monks departed. A plaque affirms it was the first place in Britain that brass was founded, in 1565. By the 17th century iron furnaces and forges were operating along the Angidy stream, a tributary of the Wye. Remains of iron-works here are preserved and worth a short detour. Display panels highlight their history and development from 1669 to 1826. At Tintern the waymarked route passes the Abbey Mill Craft Shop and Tea-room, which stands on the site of the Lower Forge. Within the mill complex is a derelict water wheel, a single survivor of approximately twenty that powered these former industries.

Raw materials and finished products were transported by packhorses along the cobbled tracks, or carried by barges from the dock at Tintern. In 1876 communications were revolutionised with the opening of the Wye Valley Railway, connecting Chepstow to Monmouth. A short branch line, constructed across the Wye served Tintern's Wire and Tinplate Works until trading ceased in 1901. The former railway bridge now serves as a useful crossing for walkers and visitors. In common with many small railways, the Wye Valley line was never successful and ceased in 1964 with 'Dr Beeching's Axe'. It's story can be traced from a display at the Old Station at Tintern, where the former booking office, platform, signal box, railway track and static coaches have been converted into a pleasant picnic site with information centre, displays and refreshment room.

Between the Abbey ruins and the Old Station the Wye Valley Walk winds through Tintern passing gift shops, antique galleries, inns, hotels and the riverside church of St Michael. Built on an ancient Celtic site the present building dates from a reconstruction of 1846. A glance to the left reveals rows of shrubs growing on the hill. This is Tintern Parva Vineyard covering six and a half acres. The owners planted the vines in 1979 and picked picked grapes from various

German vine types, including Bacchus, and Muller Thurgau, bred to produce wine in inhospitable areas. English wine producers often claim that the Romans first planted vines here, but there is not the scrap of evidence to support this theory. There is, however, documentation extant that medieval monks did make wine to celebrate Mass. This would have been opaque stuff, sweetened by honey and tasting rather like poor sherry. Today's Tintern wine is pleasant, perfumed and light, and may be purchased from the farm.

Tintern is an excellent place to start or finish a day's ramble. The Information Centre at the Old Station sells books and leaflets describing a selection of routes, enabling exploration of this scenic section of the Wye Valley. Inviting paths lead in all directions to the Devil's Pulpit with its legendary tales, Offa's Dyke, the 8th century earthwork, and to Chapel Hill where the remains of St Mary's, rebuilt in 1886, can be investigated. Waymarked routes follow the Tintern Trail to the Angidy Iron Works, the Monk's Path to Brockweir, and the Flower Patch Trail in memory of Flora Klickman.

Klickman, born in 1867, split her time between the hubbub of London and her isolated home at Brockweir. She became editor of the Girls' Own Paper and the Woman's Magazine at the beginning of the century, featured Brockweir and Tintern in her Flower Patch books. She was a spirited individual whose stories and anecdotes of the Wye Valley died with her in 1958. Recent efforts to revive her reputation resulted in an exhibition of her life and work in 1988 at the Old Station, Tintern.

From the Old Station the waymarked path leads along a former section of the Wye Valley Railway to Brockweir Bridge, an iron structure built in 1906 which replaced a ferry. Brockweir is an attractive riverside village with an inn, store, pottery and an unusual Moravian Chapel, where Flora Klickman's grave may be found. Alongside the river are remains of old quays where supplies from sailing barges, known locally as trows, were loaded and unloaded: goods destined for places upstream were transferred onto flat bottomed boats pulled by teams of men. Up to the end of the last century Brockweir's inhabitants were mainly employed as boat builders and watermen, providing the skills needed to navigate the tidal Wye with its rise and fall of twelve feet.

At the western end of Brockweir Bridge the Wye Valley Walk makes a sudden ascent, then pleasantly meanders through the woods of Coed Beddick, Botany Bay and Whitestone, where a secluded picnic site and play area are a child's delight. Short forest trails lead through spruce and fir plantations to unexpectedly beautiful views of the Wye Valley below, and the Tall Trees Walk is suitable for the disabled. In the Jubilee Grove other species of trees were planted in 1979, they include oak, cherry, sweet chestnut, beech and larch. The principal attraction of this section of the Walk, especially during inclement weather, are the Cleddon Falls which leap and bound over boulders down a misty atmospheric ravine, a spectacular sight. To view the falls descend a delightful twisting route through the gorge, established as a tourist attraction in Victorian times. Although not on the official path, Llandogo is near enough for long distance walkers to avail themselves of its accommodation and refreshment facilities and regular bus service. Llandogo was important in the days of river navigation, but now only a few house and inn names hint of its connection with the river. Near the Wye stands a church dedicated to St Oudoceus. The building was expensively restored by the Victorian architect J.P.Seddon whose name is linked with other Wye Valley churches. Nearby the river is spanned by a graceful iron bridge at Bigsweir, built to carry the turnpike road in the late 1820s. From here a network of lanes and paths lead to St Briavels on the opposite bank, where an impressive Norman castle serves as a Youth Hostel.

In 1798, the poet, William Wordsworth, stayed at Llandogo while on a walking tour with his sister Dorothy. The beauty of the Wye inspired him to write 'Lines Composed a Few Miles above Tintern Abbey', which was rushed to the printers for inclusion in his first volume of Lyrical Ballads published that year. When they reached Goodrich, Wordsworth met a young cottage girl whom he immortalised in his poem 'We are Seven'. An earlier visit to Tintern in 1793 was not so fortunate. While walking with other poets Wordsworth had a fierce argument with Robert Southey, when the party including Samuel Taylor Coleridge, lost their way home and where forced to stay the night at Tintern.

Cleddon Hall (previously known as Ravenscroft) at Llandogo, was the birthplace of Bertrand Russell, philosopher, mathematician, politician, Nobel Prize winner and campaigner against nuclear armaments. Born here in 1872, Russell was the son of Lord and Lady Amberley, eccentric and independently minded parents derided locally for there unconventional lifestyle. After a tragic early childhood, Russell aged 4, was sent to live with his grand-parents at Pembroke Lodge in Richmond Park, where he met Queen Victoria and almost every notable person of that time. It was not until 1955 that as a hyper-active octogenarian this vigorous Victorian returned to the country of his birth.

From the summit of Cleddon Falls the Wye Valley Walk continues through beech and bluebell woods to Pen-y-Fan, where once lads and lassies gathered on the green to celebrate May Day and other festivities. A short distance from here lies Manor Wood, where the Forestry Commission has laid out a forest trail leading through plantations of beech, ash, oak and larch to a viewpoint overlooking the Whitebrook valley.

At Whitebrook, wire making was carried out between 1606 and 1720. From about 1760 papermills named Fernside, Sunnyside, Clearwater, Wye Valley and the Glyn were established along the busy stream, its crystal clear water being an essential ingredient in the making of paper. The finished article was transported from Whitebrook in barges along the Wye to Bristol. The industry continued till the end of the 19th century, when the mills were gradually converted into dwellings. With their overgrown ponds they are now a picturesque sight.

From Whitebrook to Penalt the long distance path closely follows the banks of the Wye, mainly along the disused track of the Wye Valley Railway. Penalt is fairly inaccessible and overlooks the Wye from a height of 600 feet, where its tranquilly sighted church with an unusual 13th century tower occupies a magnificent position. In the 1820s this area was renowned for mill stones made from local Pudding Stone, a hard conglomerate rock containing a mass of quartz pebbles resembling suet puddling. Fragments of these millstones can still be seen strewn among the ferns.

Famous members of the Fabian Society visited this area after the society's formation in 1885. Among them were Beatrice Webb, social reformer and writer, whose father lived at The Argoed, her husband Sydney Webb, historian and statesman, and Irish wit and dramatist George Bernard Shaw. Like Bertrand Russell, these talented Victorian campaigners lived long and useful lives spanning nearly a century of dramatic change.

Besides the river at Penalt stands the Boat Inn, a reminder that this isolated place was served by ferry conveying both horse and foot passengers across the water from Redbrook. Communications were improved in 1876 when the Wye Valley Railway passed through this remote parish: although the line was closed in 1964, a rusting 300 foot long viaduct remains. A footbridge alongside carries the Wye Valley Walk across to Redbrook, from Wales to England.

At Redbrook walkers can join the Offa's Dyke Path. This 168 mile long distance path established in 1971 celebrates the 8th century dyke thrown up by order of King Offa to demarcate the Welsh and Mercian boundary. The National Trail runs through the ancient frontier from Chepstow to Prestatyn. At its southern end it hugs the banks of the Wye through Gloucestershire, where remains of this ancient linear earthwork can still be seen. Combined with the Wye Valley Walk these two fine waymarked paths provide walkers with some excellent circular routes.

From the early 17th century Redbrook boasted an active past and the industrial archeologist will have no difficulty in locating sites of former furnaces, forges, mills, a brewery, a tramway with an incline bridge, a railway track and a warehouse with wharves by the river. Above the village is the Forest of Dean,

TINTERN ABBEY.

where iron ore was readily available. For a while smelting was carried out by the English Copper Company founded in 1691, but these works were recorded as ruins in 1827. Tin plating was more successful and it continued until 1961, by which time this was the last traditional tin-plate factory in Britain.

For over 300 years forge, foundry and furnace work took place beside the bridge, but only remains at Redbrook and a few tools and photographs at Monmouth Museum are reminders of this industrial past. Now the dirt and dust have settled, Redbrook is a quiet riverside village with a modest and crumbling church dedicated to St Saviour, designed in 1873 by the London architect J.P.Seddon. A few inns and guest houses offer refreshments and accommodation.

In the 18th century the fishing rights below Redbrook were controlled by great landowners who sent their catches of salmon to the market at Bristol and London. Nowadays salmon are caught each year by a large number of anglers who require licences from the National Rivers Authority and permission from those owning the fishing rights. The relatively pure waters of the Wye support twenty nine species of fish, including salmon, trout, chubb, dace, pike, roach and eels; salmon vary in size from four to forty pounds, good sized trout are found in upper reaches.

From Redbrook to Monmouth the Wye Valley Walk follows the riverside for 3 miles along a delightful stretch with a variety of wild flowers, including masses of comfrey, campion and vetches, and on sunny days dragonflies hover colourfully above the rippling currents. The ubiquitous swan peacefully co-exist with families of duck, stalking herons, the shy kingfisher and beady-eyed cormorant. The river provides an ever changing scene. Wading cows lap from the cool water, fishermen patiently wait for a bite, groups of canoeists energetically paddle their way downstream.

From Redbrook the more active walker may prefer to follow Offa's Dyke Path to Monmouth which climbs 800 feet to The Kymin. Here a Naval Temple and Round House overlook the town of Monmouth set against a range of distant, misty hills. In the 1790s young bucks from Monmouth assembled to erect a summer house. When it was completed wine-soaked meals were enjoyed in an upper banqueting room, from the windows of which diners gazed upon magnificent views. Games were played upon the bowling green and scenic walks were followed through Beaulieu Grove.

The recently restored Naval Temple commemorates sixteen British Admirals of the late 18th century. Familiar heroes like Nelson, Boscawen, Hood and Hawk are on the medallions among others less famous. This unusual monument was opened in 1801 with much

24

ceremony. Dancing followed breakfast, with further entertainment in Monmouth. When Admiral Lord Nelson toured the Wye Valley in 1802 he visited The Kymin and Monmouth and this established the great mariner's connection with the town.

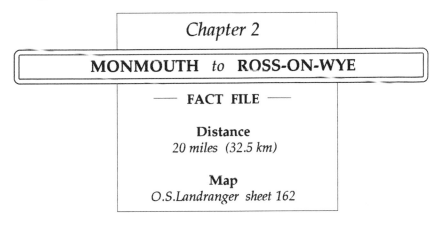

Chapter 2

MONMOUTH *to* ROSS-ON-WYE

—— FACT FILE ——

Distance
20 miles (32.5 km)

Map
O.S.Landranger sheet 162

Transport
There is a regular bus service operating between Monmouth and Ross-on-Wye (except Sundays) with occasional buses to Symonds Yat. For further information ☎ 0989 62319 or write to the Engineering and Planning Officer, Hereford and Worcester County Council, Spetchley Road, Worcester, WR5 2NP. Two ferries cross the Wye at Symonds Yat except in adverse weather conditions. ☎ 0600 890435 and 0600 890232.

Parking
Monmouth, The Biblins, Symonds Yat East and West, Lower Lydbrook, Goodrich Castle, Kerne Bridge and Wilton Road at Ross-on-Wye.

Picnic Sites
Official sites are at Symonds Yat East, Lower Lydbrook, Kerne Bridge and Goodrich Castle with some provision on the riverside at Ross-on-Wye.

Refreshments
Monmouth, Symonds Yat East and West, Goodrich, Glewstone, Walford and Ross-on-Wye.

Accommodation and general visitor information
Tourist Information Centres at:
Monmouth ☎ 0600 713899
Ross-on-Wye ☎ 0989 562768

Camp Sites
Monmouth, Christchurch, Symonds Yat East and West, Upper Lydbrook, Goodrich and Wilton at Ross-on-Wye.

Youth Hostels
Monmouth and Welsh Bicknor
Youth Hostels Association ☎ *0727 855215.*

Circular Walks
Waymarked routes from Monmouth, Symonds Yat, Lydbrook, Goodrich
and Nature Trails in the Forest of Dean.

The Countryside Service
Wye Valley A.O.N.B., Hadnock Road, Monmouth
☎ *0600 713977.*

Public Telephone
Monmouth, Crocker's Ash, Symonds Yat East and West, Lower Lydbrook,
Kerne Bridge, Goodrich, Coughton and Ross-on-Wye.

Public Toilets
Monmouth, Symonds Yat East and West, Lower Lydbrook, Kerne Bridge,
Goodrich and Ross-on-Wye.

☞ **ROUTE DIRECTIONS** ☜

Cross the Wye into **Monmouth**: a subway leads under the busy **A40** to the town centre. The route follows the west bank past a display board and the **Monmouth Rowing Club**. Proceed to **Dixton** via a variety of swing gates, stiles and footbridges leading through riverside meadows.

From this ancient white-washed church the path hugs the river then forks right to cross the **Mally Brook**. Further upstream a stile leads into scrubland near the site of **Chapel Farm**. Below the overgrown embankments of the A40 the path crosses the Welsh Border into Herefordshire, around the secluded **Vaga Cottage**, keeping close to the Wye as it sweeps away from the intrusive A40.

The path skirts the landscaped grounds of **Wyestone Leys** with its Victorian mansion, recording studio and deer park, accompanying the Wye as it winds through a picturesque gorge. Wooded slopes of the **Little Doward** reach down to the riverside, with the bald rocky crags of **The Seven Sisters** frowning down from the **Great Doward**. The way twists and turns attractively between trees and saplings passing another waymarked route to **King Arthur's Cave**.

Cross water meadows at **The Biblins** with its unattractive **Youth Adventure Centre** and unusual suspension bridge conveying Wye Valley walkers across the river. For an alternative route to **Symonds Yat** remain on the west bank and cross the river by ferry to rejoin the **Wye Valley Walk** at **Symonds Yat East**.

After crossing the swaying bridge turn left through the scenic gorge following the remains of the **Ross to Monmouth Railway**. Continue to **New Weir** with its flurry of white water, then **Symonds Yat** with its odd assortment of inns, tea-rooms, guest houses and hotels. To enjoy the spectacular view from **Yat Rock** follow the steeply ascending waymarked path by the **Royal Hotel**: the **Wye Valley Walk** can be re-joined after a short descent.

The main route continues from the **Royal Hotel** through **Yat East** and along the river to its second ferry crossing. Here it bears right and climbs through woods, across two minor roads and bearing right around **Huntsham Hill** with fine views of **Goodrich** and **Coppet Hill**. At the brow do not miss a left turn, descend a few steps, continue along a pleasant path down to the river at the other side of this horseshoe bend.

From this tranquil setting the path leaves the river, veering right and climbing between leaning trees, massive boulders and ruined buildings. Cross straight over the forest track until the path turns sharp left, directed by a signpost, a quarter of a mile below the 500 foot high **Yat Rock**. This narrow, rocky, slippery path leads to an isolated cottage before turning right along the dismantled remains of the railway line. The river and path gently meander together through another picturesque gorge, between imperious **Coldwell Rocks** and the thick woods on **Coppet Hill**. Beyond a small stone barn glance towards the opposite bank to observe the **Warre Monument**. Further on, in spring the embankment is lined with a rich profusion of delicate flowers flourishing in this sunny and sheltered spot. Cross the stile, negotiate a flight of steps and another stile, and veer left to the riverside path which leads through arable fields to the paper works at **Lower Lydbrook**. A disused railway viaduct carries the **Wye Valley Walk** across the river from **Gloucestershire** back into **Herefordshire**.

The path continues upstream following a grassy bank below **Welsh Bicknor Youth Hostel**, church and churchyard, a lovely sight in spring when carpeted with daffodils. Now the river is pursued through meadows and ploughed fields for about 1½ miles, around another **Wye** loop below **Courtfield**, on the opposite bank, the outline of **Bishopwood** appears.

A stile gives entry to **Thomas Wood**, where there are further remains of the railway. A remote cottage is passed before a diverted route leads above the original eroding riverside path. From the edge of the woods there is an attractive preview of **Goodrich Castle**, **Flanesford Priory** and **Kerne Bridge**. Keep

MONMOUTH *to* ROSS-ON-WYE

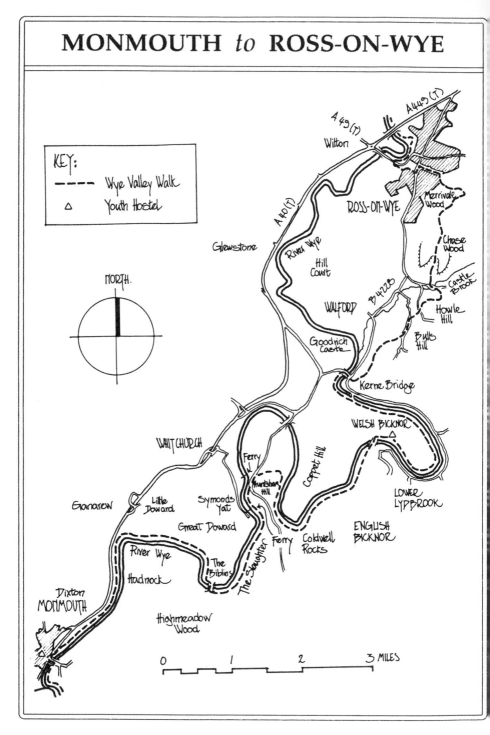

KEY:
- - - - Wye Valley Walk
△ Youth Hostel

NORTH.

A 49 (T)
A449 (T)
Wilton
A 40 (T)
ROSS-ON-WYE
Merrivale Wood
Glewstone
River Wye
Hill Court
Chase Wood
Castle Brook
B 4228
WALFORD
Howle Hill
Bulls Hill
Goodrich Castle
Kerne Bridge
WELSH BICKNOR
WHITCHURCH
Ferry
Coppet Hill
Huntsham Hill
LOWER LYPBROOK
Ganarew
Little Doward
Symonds Yat
Great Doward
ENGLISH BICKNOR
The Slaughter Ferry
Coldwell Rocks
River Wye
The Biblins
Hadnock
Dixton
MONMOUTH
Highmeadow Wood

0   1   2   3 MILES

beside the Wye through riverside meadows and cross **Kerne Bridge** where an unexpected right turn leads to **Kerne Bridge Picnic Site.**

Cross the road by the bus shelter, follow a tarmac lane, then turn left up a track, between cottages; the beginning of an energetic stretch over **Bulls, Leys, Howle** and **Chase Hills.** A zig zagging path lined with beech trees ascends the first hill before turning left along a track passing cottages. Keep left and descend a leafy path with wayside quarries and wonderful views. Upon touching the road at **Walford** opposite a saw mill, bear right following a track above the rapidly expanding village. Beyond a stone dwelling, fork right, following a shaded path to **Springherne** on **Bulls Hill.** The route crosses the road. On the left of **Bulls Hill Cottage,** steps lead to a stile. Descend the meadow to a stream and up to the left hand corner where an enclosed path leads onto theroad at **Howle Hill.**

Cross the road and follow a bridle-way around **Hill House** to a crossways at **Still Meadow Cottage.** Take the left fork to **Rose Cottage,** a stileon the left leads into a paddock. Bear right at a line of trees above an old sunken lane, cross the series of stiles at the bottom then walk across the meadow to join the road at **Coughton.**

Turn left through the pretty valley, and beyond farm buildings turn right through fields and gates to the woods of **Chase Hill.** This final ascent before **Ross-on-Wye,** twists and turns between trees and boulders, passing through a conifer plantation, then bearing right onto a forest track.

At the top of this 600 foot climb, a level track ahead leads below the ramparts of an Iron Age hill-fort, there is a pleasant descent to pass **Hill Farm** and skirt **Merrivale Wood.** A stile leads out of these woods onto a field path, bear left to **Alton Court Woods** and over a stile into **Tank Meadow** with its 19th century reservoir. There are fine views of **Ross-on-Wye** on the approach to a gate on the left, where a path leads to **Alton Court.**

From the outskirts of **Ross-on-Wye,** the **Wye Valley Walk** is waymarked around the town. From **Alton Court** follow a tarmac lane to its junction with **Alton Street,** turn left to the cross-roads at **Copse Cross.** If refreshments or accommodation are required turn right into the town, otherwise go left passing **Toll Cottage** in **Walford Road.** Beyond the sports ground at **Crossfields** turn right along **Ashfield Park Road** leading to a private road. Follow this to **Rectory Farm** bearing left along an enclosed path to a swing gate. Descend a few steps, turn right, then left, taking the right hand fork down shallow steps to the **Wilton Road** car park.

Between Monmouth and Ross-on-Wye the river winds its way through a dramatic gorge with towering limestones bluffs and hills cloaked with hanging woods. This untamed and virtually unknown beauty of the Wye attracted 18th century writers and artists seeking the 'Picturesque'. At the turn of the 18th and 19th centuries the study of visual values was reflected in English literature, painting and landscape: Sir Uvedale Price, a great enthusiast, from Foxley, wrote a three volumed essay expounding its virtues in 1786.

The woods, rocks and water of the Wye Valley provided natural artistic views which greatly appealed to followers of the Picturesque. These include Gray, Gilpin, Wathem, Ireland, Heath, Bloomfield, Twamley, Fosbroke, Roscoe and Ritchie who left vivid written and pictorial accounts of the Wye's glorious scenery as viewed from their pleasure boats. This trip along the river became known as the Wye Tour, and started in 1745 when the Rev. John Egerton became Rector of Ross, for he often entertained his wealthy friends and relatives with a boat trip down the Wye. His notable guests were so impressed by the discovery of such hidden beauty that it created a fashion later commercialised by boat proprietors, and inn-keepers; crafts with provisions and crew were hired at Monmouth or Ross for an excursion to Chepstow. The leisurely journey allowed time to write, sketch, picnic and explore on foot the scenery interrupted with busy industrial scenes at New Weir, Lydbrook and Bishopswood.

Towards the end of the 18th century when the Napoleonic Wars disrupted European travel, erstwhile travellers in search of 'Picturesque Beauty' turned their attention nearer home, which led to the popularity of the 'Wye Tour'. The fashion continued into this century, despite the opening of the railways and improvements made to the highways, with Ross and Monmouth established as desirable tourist centres.

The Wye Valley Walk approaches Monmouth by the early 17th century Wye Bridge. This ancient border town is well worth a visit if only to learn of its history. Whilst the Romans inhabited this place, Monmouth's tangible past really became apparent under the Normans whose strategy was to take advantage of its well defended position between the Wye and Monnow, establishing a market town with a castle and Benedictine Priory, although little of these remain. The 13th century fortified bridge over the Monnow is the most emphatic structural survivor reflecting the town's medieval stature. Distinguished names associated with Monmouth include the 12th century historian, Geoffrey of Monmouth, King Henry V born at the castle in 1387, Lord Nelson who visited the town in 1802, and Charles Rolls, the renown aviator and co-founder of Rolls Royce, born nearby in 1877. Outside an impressive 1724 Shire Hall are statues of Henry V and Charles Rolls. An oriel window is erroneously called Geoffrey's Window at the Priory site, now used as a Youth Hostel, and Nelson name is commemorated by a museum, where a unique collection of his memorabilia can be seen.

Other places of historical interest are the eerie and derelict slaughterhouses built as a series of arches supporting Priory Street in 1837 by the Monmouth Turnpike Trustees to relieve the town's traffic congestion. Nearby Tibbs Bridge (footbridge), leads over the Monnow into Vauxhall, with its late 18th century pleasure gardens laid out by John Tibbs the landlord of the Beaufort Arms: under him this coaching inn flourished, but its days of hospitality are over, the premises have been converted into an attractive shopping mews.

Monmouth suffered no shortage of inns for tired travellers and weary carriers using the network of routes from London to South Wales. Roads were in a deplorable state until improvements were gradually made by the Monmouth Turnpike Trust established in 1755. From around this time the town was surrounded by turn-pike gates at which coaches, carriages and wagons paid a toll towards the upkeep of the highways. Those travelling to Hereford or Ross paid their tolls at Monkgate or Dixton-gate where toll houses have survived, although now converted to private dwellings.

Several talented historians have written at length about Monmouth, including Archdeacon Coxe and Sir J.A.Bradney, but the most important are Charles Heath, antiquarian bookseller, printer and mayor at the turn of the 19th century, and more recently Keith Kissack, retired museum curator, councillor and magistrate. Their carefully researched books and pamphlets can be consulted at the newly housed library at the Rolls Hall, a building donated to the town in 1887 by Lord Llangattock, father of Charles Rolls. Monmouth's 'lost' history is currently being unearthed by members of the Monmouth Archaeological Society, excavating centuries of silt and rubbish to unearth Roman, Saxon, Norman and Medieval artefacts.

St Mary's churchyard is worth a visit to inspect headstones left standing after an official 'tidy up'. One inscription sends a chill up the spine, it reads ominously: 'Reader only stand and think, That I am in eternity, and thou art on the brink'. Another is dedicated to a man who traded as a saddler and pawnbroker, while a further unusual example must have proved a nightmare for the stone mason. It appears like a crossword with a mass of letters which cleverly play on the deceased man's name. A heavy, dull monument commemorates the town's printer and writer, Charles Heath, who died in 1831, aged 70. At his shop in Agincourt Square, (surely worth a plaque), he was visited by Lord Nelson in 1802, when Heath gave some of his books to the admiral.

Monmouth remains, Anglicised, although firmly established in Wales by local government re-organisation in the 1970s. The bustling market town has a relaxing and comfortable atmosphere where a selection of inns, hotels, guest-houses and tea rooms offer welcome refreshment and hospitality. A variety of shops are clustered around Church Street and Agincourt Square, and line the wide thoroughfare leading down to the Monnow Bridge.

At Monmouth walkers can join Offa's Dyke Path, next encountered by the Wye Valley Walk at Hay-on-Wye, or follow shorter way-marked routes to Newton Court, Buckholt Wood and Wonaston Church. However, the Wye Valley Walk proceeds along the west side of the Wye through riverside meadows to St Peter's Church at Dixton, a pretty white-washed building with a small broach spire. Inside brass tablets indicate flooding levels of five to six feet in 1929, 1947 and 1960, although earlier aquatic disasters which disrupted church services are also recorded. A window in the chancel commemorates the last chapel of St Michael at Chapel Farm in Gararew. The farm buildings were demolished during the construction of the A40 in the 1960s. Interesting headstones and monuments to the Griffin family from Newton and Hadnock are reminders that the church served communities on both sides of the River Wye. St Peter's was yet another of J.P.Seddon's restorations in 1861 after flood damage caused in 1852. The riverside path crosses the border into Herefordshire, passing the site of Chapel Farm and around the picturesque Vaga Cottage. Just beyond this isolated dwelling a flight of stone steps steeply ascends to the dual carriageway, all that remains of winding walks through the woods laid out in the late 18th century. From here the path veers away from the intrusive main road and follows the Wye as it meanders through the landscaped grounds of Wyestone Leys. This Victorian mansion and contemporary recording studio are superbly sited, sheltered by the Little Doward and overlooking the river with in the distance the shaggy mane of the Forest of Dean.

A house built at the Leys in 1795, was purchased in 1820 by Richard Blakemore, an ironmaster and Member of Parliament from South Wales. He re-built the mansion with materials ferried across the Wye from the remains of Hadnock House which was being demolished, he further 'improved' his new estate by pulling down cottages, building roads, establishing a deer park and adding a lodge. All this was done to the detriment of cottagers who lost their homes and grazing rights on the Little Doward: contemporary accounts suggest they were tricked out of their dwellings by this wily industrialist, although Blakemore was reported as being a benevolent employer and generous to the poor.

The site of an Iron Age hill-fort on the Little Doward was damaged by Blakemore when he erected a curious iron tower in the 1840s. It was said to be seventy feet high commanding a fine view of the surrounding counties. This unsightly folly became unsafe and was dismantled in the 1920s. Its former site is covered with forestry plantations laid out in 1953 to form the letters 'ER' commemorating the Coronation of Her Majesty Queen Elizabeth II. After Blakemore's death in 1855 the Leys passed to his nephew who then sold it to John Bannerman, a textile manufacturer from Manchester, who appears to have added Wyestone to the name.

On the Little Doward a character known as Slippery Jim survived as a hermit: his simple dwelling shared with his wife was a cave camouflaged with leaves and turves. They made a meagre living selling crystals and fossils to visitors in the 1870s when it was reported that the pair neither washed nor brushed their hair and dressed in filthy rags.

The Woodland Trust has recently purchased the Little Doward, now designated part of the Upper Wye Gorge Site of Special Scientific Interest (SSSI). In springtime these woods are a wonderful sight, bluebells interspersed with patches of white wood anemones and wild garlic growing in profusion below a 'forest' of beech, oak, ash and coppiced hazel. On the higher slopes an enticing grassy ride encircles the remains of a hill-fort and ancient yews cling to massive rocky outcrops which have been weathered into gullies and gaping caves. This limestone soil also supports the rare fingered and dwarf sedges, bloody cranesbill, whitebeam, large leaved lime and spindle. The Trust plan public access along a network of paths to scenic viewpoints.

The Wye Valley Walk follows the river below the Little Doward and in front of a cottage built in the picturesque style which once housed the estate kennels. Stone ruins are the remnants of fish houses, where freshly caught salmon were smoked. This quiet stretch is an ideal place to study wildlife. A small island in mid-river provides an undisturbed nesting site for swans, moorhens and coots. There are tracks and signs of fallow deer, mink and badger. Whilst for the ornothologist buzzards, warblers, ravens, pied fly-catchers and peregrine falcons frequent this part of the Wye gorge, where fast stretches of water attract grey wagtail and the common sandpiper and a flash of the colourful, but discreet, kingfisher may be glimpsed. Along eroding banks alders and willows, which have collapsed into the river, somehow survive with roots perilously clinging to the banks against the Wye's swift currents. The opposite side of the river is covered with deciduous and coniferous plantations. Highmeadow Woods are managed by the Forestry Commission. Here, between rows of conifers, stand exceptionally fine oaks, limes, yews and ash: notably the Gosling Ash, named after Sir Arthur Gosling, former Director General of the Forestry Commission, this, his favourite tree, the tallest broadleaf in the Forest of Dean, reaching a height of 108 feet.

Lady Park Wood, designated a National Nature Reserve by English Nature, unmanaged woodland has been enclosed so that it may be undisturbed and its natural changes monitored.

An energetic trail leads through Highmeadow Woods to some remarkable natural features. Near Harkening Rock is a huge conglomerate rock with an overhang which it is said aided game-keepers whilst 'harkening' for poachers stalking fallow deer (which still inhabit these woods). The Suck Stone, is an enormous sand-stone boulder estimated to weigh at least 12,000 tons. The Buck Stone with its Druidical legend originally rocked until van-dalised by local youths in 1885; at a height of 915 feet above the Wye gorge, this site offers tremendous views notably towards the dark horizon of the Black Mountains.

This delightful gorge is guarded by the Seven Sisters, a row of limestone spires. These bluffs, dipping towards the river, were formed when joints in the Crease Limestone were opened thus causing some blocks to fall. The feature was undercut by the Wye, when it flowed at a higher level than it does today.

The forest trail leads along the heads of the Seven Sisters where exceptional views may be admired, *take great care*. The trail continues through the Great Doward woods to King Arthur's Cave and other weathered hollows. When the floor of King Arthur's Cave was excavated in 1870 archaeologists found bone points and flint knives, evidence of Stone Age occupation. They also discovered jaw bones and the teeth of the cave bear, woolly rhinoceros and mammoth. Samples of these are exhibited in Hereford City Museum.

Leeping Stocks, a small 20 acre reserve managed by Hereford Nature Trust, lies hidden amid the maze of criss-crossing lanes and tracks on Great Doward. Originally small fields divided by stone walls and beech hedges it is now the habitat for a wide variety of fauna and flora. From a path decorated with early primroses an unexpected picture of the Wye Valley appears framed by silver birches. The Great Doward was the site of extensive quarrying and lime burning, but the only industry remaining is the manufacturing of concrete products. A Rural Heritage Centre displays a collection of vintage tractors and horse-drawn vehicles together with agricultural machinery and bygone utensils.

A wooded, gorge below the two Dowards widens at The Biblins, where fertile meadows are used as a camp site. The Wye Valley Walk crosses the river via a narrow suspension bridge, which only six people at a time should cross. The wire mesh bridge constructed by the Forestry Commission in 1957 replaced an earlier ropeway thus enabling forestry workers to cross the river thus avoiding a long detour. On the eastern bank walkers follow the disused track of the Ross to Monmouth railway. The line, in use from 1873-1965, provided a scenic nourney along one of the most attractive stretches of the Wye Valley. The Slaughter, are steep cliffs above the river, colourfully misrepresented in local legend as the scene of a battle between the Romans and the Celts.

The sound of rushing water heralds the rapids at New Weir, where canoeists' skills are tested by white water. Opposite the small island was the site of a forge which operated from the 17th century to the early 1800s. The Partridge family, ironmasters, who worked the furnaces at Bishopswood, leased the New Weir forge from 1753 and manufactured iron here till 1798. The works provided a different and perhaps exciting scene for the early Wye

Symonds Yat Ferry.

tourists. Great volumes of smoke issued from the forge, worked noisily by iron hammers powered by the river which thundered over the weir. When the iron works were abandoned the buildings fell into decay leaving only a few scanty and silent remains.

New Weir starts the Wye's famous three mile loop around the Yat Rock, a towering promontory of Lower Dolomite standing at over 500 feet. The hamlets of Symonds Yat East and West make a pretty picture of inns, hotels and tea rooms along the water's edge with white-washed cottages peeping from wooded hillsides. The natural beauty has been spoilt by recent unsympathetic commercialisation with the establishment of needless tourist attractions. Boat trips offer visitors a sedate view of the gorge while more adventurous canoeists slide by. Two ferries still cross the river by an ancient system of ropes and cables, a pleasant reminder of former days, an experience to be savoured.

From Yat East a zig-zagging path ascends the summit of Yat Rock. This famous panoramic viewpoint that has attracted tourists since the dawn of 'Picturesque' appreciation in the 18th century, and remains, in common perception, as one of the 'great' views of the Wye. To cater for the late 20th century tourist various facilities are on hand, a rustic log cabin selling teas, ices, guidebooks and post-cards, and a recently extended car park. The Yat Rock provides a lofty platform from which to observe the agile peregrine falcons, re-occupying nesting sites on the magnificent cliffs formed by Coldwell Rocks. Peregrine are smaller than the buzzard, with pointed wings, a long tail and streamlined head with a hooked bill. They are amongst the world's fastest fliers, and utilise rapid wing beats with alternative glides and dives to catch pigeons, bats and insects. During the spring and summer when their chicks are greatly at risk the Royal Society for the Protection of Birds (RSPB) and the Forestry Commission keep a constant eye on them. A telescope is at hand for the public to watch the antics of these beautiful and fascinating birds of prey.

Far below Yat Rock the river meanders past Whitchurch with its pretty riverside church dedicated to Dubricius, a local saint. Iron-works were established here at Old Forge before being moved to New Weir. Further on, the river is crossed by Huntsham Bridge, built in 1885 by the Vaughans from Courtfield, replacing a ford and ferry known as Hunts-Holm Rope. Nearby stands Huntsham Court, a mellow Jacobean building surrounded by high walls where the Wye Valley Farm Park is now sited. An extensive Roman villa was discovered in the river meadows during the 1960s: The Queen Stone, a prehistoric standing stone, marks an earlier site.

From Huntsham Hill the Wye Valley Walk descends a rocky, well worn path between large boulders and ruined dwellings shaded by a variety of standing and fallen trees smothered in Old Man's Beard. Near the river squats an enormous boulder, of Puddling Stone, the size and shape of a cottage; as a wildlife habitat it supports mosses, ferns, ivy and Herb Robert, while insects, birds and mice make homes with dried leaves in its crevices.

Another spectacular gorge is formed as the Wye winds between the long ridge of Coppet Hill and the craggy outcrop of Coldwell Rocks. Although the path runs just below the Yat Rock with its unfailing stream of visitors, this stretch is particularly peaceful. Peregrines soar above, fallow deer silently graze the slopes of Coppet Hill, startled pheasants periodically ring the air with their sharp squawking, woodpeckers dart from tree to tree and waterfowl inhabit the calm waters. In spring blue and white violets, yellow primroses, wood anemones and wild garlic are followed by bluebells, great mullein and barren strawberry. In sheltered spots orange tip, wood white and tortoiseshell butterflies are enticed out by the sun.

The disused track of the Ross to Monmouth railway is rejoined along the river bank below the impressive cliffs of Coldwell. On the opposite bank, almost hidden in the scrub of Coldwell Woods, is a monument commemorating a tragedy. In 1804, while picnicking with his parents, 15 year old John Whitehead Warre, born in Oporto and related to the famous Port shippers, was drowned while attempting to swim across the river. In spite of the boatman's valiant efforts. In sorrow and gratitude the boy's father, through Charles Heath, presented Smith, the boatman, and a helpful cottager with inscribed silver tankards; shortly after this unfortunate event Smith died after selling his silver cup to the landlord of the Swan Inn at Ross.

The Wye Valley Walk continues below Rosemary Topping a conical hill. From the riverside two pleasant footpaths ascend to the Gloucestershire village of English Bicknor, where one or two houses offer bed and breakfast. The ancient church of St Mary stands within the earthworks of an early castle over looking a preserved section of Offa's Dyke, at this point divorced from the long distance path. Features of note include three 13th centuries effigies, a beautifully carved Norman arch and a chapel dedicated to the Machen family. In spring the lane to Common Grove is fringed with an abundance of brightly coloured flowers. A signposted path from here leads to the top of Coldwell Rocks, where individually named cliffs may be explored.

Behind the factory at Lower Lydbrook a disused railway viaduct, a remnant of the defunct Ross to Monmouth line, carries the Wye Valley

Walk across the river to Welsh Bicknor formerly in Monmouthshire, but now reverted to Herefordshire. Before leaving Lydbrook it is interesting to note that from the end of the 18th century, when a coal wharf was established, it quickly became industrialised with tram roads and railways built to transport Dean Forest's products of coal, tin, iron, stone and timber. A few features of this period can be viewed from a long flight of steps which lead up to the stark abutments of a viaduct. Constructed in 1872 the former viaduct carried the Severn and Wye Railway across the Lydbrook valley at a height of 90 feet. The riverbank, where a ferry used to carry pedestrians across to Welsh Bicknor, has now been converted into an attractive picnic site. Cottages and inn names reflect its industrial heritage e.g Mill Row.

Welsh Bicknor is encircled by a scenic meander of the Wye. The old Victorian rectory is now a Youth Hostel and the original parsonage lies in ruins beside St Margaret's Church. An attractive re-building of 1858, it contains an effigy, which at one time was thought to represent the Countess of Salisbury who nursed the infant Henry V at Courtfield. This mansion later became the home of the Vaughans, a Catholic family who re-built the house in Georgian times and added a Victorian chapel.

From Welsh Bicknor the walk clings to the riverbank for nearly 3 miles through meadows and woods below Courtfield and Coppet Hill. While exploring this stretch a backward glance reveals a superb view of Ruardean church with its splendid 14th century spire, a prominent landmark in the Forest of Dean. Also on that side of the Wye there is a forested area, Bishops Wood, and hidden amongst the trees and shrubs are remnants of forges and furnaces dating from the 16th century and acquired by John Partridge in 1822. He built Bishops Wood House, which was partially destroyed by fire in 1873, many years after the iron works ceased. During his 88 years Partridge erected the church with its simple bellcote and a school to accommodate 100 children: his untended grave lies in the secluded churchyard.

While excavating stones for road repair at Bishops Wood in 1895 workmen discovered an earthenware jar full of Roman coins. This exciting find, together with two other shattered jars had been buried on sloping ground near Partridge's school. On examination the 17,550 coins, thought to be a military hoard, were dated to the 3rd and 4th centuries: those bearing Christian symbols minted during the time of Constantine the Great are of special interest. A jar fragment and specimens of these silver-washed bronze coins may be inspected at Hereford City Museum. Before crossing the handsome 1828 stone bridge at Kerne, formerly Quern, make a short detour to explore the historic and scenic sites at Goodrich, en route passing Flanesford Priory with its original refractory, barns and fish-ponds established by the Augustinians in the 14th century, and now sympathetically converted into holiday homes. A footpath into the village leads to the top of the Dry Arch, an unusual feature constructed about the same time as Kerne Bridge. The 13th century church of St Giles, with a prominent 14th century tower and spire, is surrounded by an assortment of ancient and modern buildings.

Amongst the generations of weathered gravestones the keen eyed will locate one in memory of the artist Joshua Cristall buried in 1847 on the north side of the church. Cristall first visited the Wye Valley whilst on a sketching tour in 1802 when he produced a picture of Goodrich, but it was not until 1823 that he settled here in a cottage overlooking the churchyard. A talented and respected artist he produced sketches, oils and watercolours of classical and rural scenes including romanticised drawings of boys and girls working on Coppet Hill. A collection of his works is housed at Hereford City Art Gallery and an exhibition of his sketches and paintings were exhibited in 1992 at the Ross-on-Wye Festival of the Arts.

Unfortunately, the church at Goodrich is kept locked, a sad sign of our times. Inside the church lie the remains of Thomas Swift, vicar here during the Civil War: Swift was an active Royalist thereby causing much suffering and danger to his large family. The Parliamentarians ejected him from his living, threw him into prison and sequestrated his estate. Thomas Swift died in 1658 the same year as Oliver Cromwell, just two years before the restoration of the monarchy. Four of his sons settled in Ireland, driven there by cruel treatment and the death of their father: Jonathan Swift, Dean of St Patricks in Dublin, author of Gulliver's Travels, was one of Thomas' grandsons.

The chief feature and pride of Goodrich is the Norman castle, built by the Marcher Lords to defend the Welsh Borders and an ancient Wye crossing. The castle's strength was not tested until the Civil War when its walls were breached by the Parliamentarians in 1646 with the aid of a cannon, Roaring Meg, now on permanent display outsidethe Churchill Gardens Museum at Hereford. In 1646 Colonel Birch captured Goodrich Castle with its governor, Sir Henry Lingen, 50 gentlemen and 120 soldiers who were reported to be short of ammunition and water. Also confiscated were "30 barrels of beer, large stores of corn and meal, 60 fliches of bacon, 150 bushels of peas, a hogshead of claret, half a hogshead of sherry and a good stock of butter, cheese and beef". The castle is open most days to the public, to inspect its ruined keep, great hall, arched gateway, chapel and round towers. Whilst exploring the battlements a wonderful view of the Wye is obtained emphasising the castle's fine defensive position.

Separated from the castle by a deep dingle, sitedon another promontory was Goodrich Court built between 1828 and 1832 for Sir Samuel Rush Meyrick, to house his vast collection of armour. Edward Blore designed the fairy tale castle to produce a dramatic effect above hanging woods which reach down to the river. After the antiquarian died in 1848 the Court and contents were sold. Between 1940 and 1945 an Essex public school transferred to the mansion as did so many private institutions at this time, shortly afterwards it was demolished leaving a mock Gothic gatehouse on the Monmouth road, a lodge house and gasworks, all now used as dwellings.

Overlooking Goodrich village is the ferny spine of Coppet Hill, large Pudding Stones project above slopes of bracken, gorse, willow herb and woodland. Decaying boundary walls covered with mosses, brambles and ferns provide enticing habitats for adders. Wild flowers grow in profusion along the paths, primroses, violets, orchids, harebells and bluebells in the coppiced wood. Until quite recently there was no public access across the hill, however, since the formation of the Coppet Hill Common Trust, an attractive range of paths are maintained and waymarked by the Countryside Service, leading to a summit affording excellent views from a height of nearly 600 feet. A heap of overgrown stones is the only visible signs of an 18th century folly built as a Summer House.

From Goodrich with its village store and mock Gothic inn, the Wye Valley Walk follows an energetic scenic route traversing steep hills to Ross-on-Wye. An easier alternative is to stay on the west side of the Wye following a riverside path below the ramparts of Goodrich Castle and through Pencraig Court Woods to Glewstone Boat and Weirend, rejoining the official path at Wilton. Improvements along this section have been carried out by volunteers from the Wye Valley Countryside Service, the Ross Civic Society and Ross Rotary Club with the assistance of Hereford and Worcester County Council who supplied tools, materials and insurance cover.

Near Kerne Bridge is a newly established picnic site with parking, seats. tables, canoe launch and display panels depicting the history and wildlife of the Wye Valley. From here the Wye Valley Walk makes a rapid ascent to Leys Hill before dropping down to Walford, where a saw mill stands on the site of an earlier water powered corn mill. The place-name Walford means 'Welsh-ford' and a lane still leads to the ancient river crossing.

A white-washed cottage at Kerne Bridge overlooking the Wye was the home of Robert Pashley, whose skill as a fisherman earned him the soubriquet 'Wizard of the Wye'. Pashley was born in 1880, and between 1908 and 1947 caught 9,122 salmon and grilse in the Wye mostly from the Hill Court and Goodrich waters. He served on the parish, district and county council, the Wye Catchment Board, the Oddfellows, and the Wye Board of Conservators. When he died in 1956 Alderman Pashley bequeathed much of his £20,000 estate to fund the primary school at Walford; the village hall, which opened in 1969, bears his name.

Walford is an expanding village with a school, inn, shop, garage and church dedicated to St Michael. From the lychgate an avenue of limes leads into the graveyard where the tip of the spire stands as a reminder of damage caused by lightening: monuments include the Rev. Thomas Dudley Fosbroke, M.A., F.A.S., vicar of Walford and Ruardean for 32 years, who died on New Year's Day 1842. In the literary world he attained a degree of eminence as a scholar, anti-quarian and local historian. His books include a guide to the Wye Tour and a useful account of Goodrich Court written in the first half of the 19th century.

From the church a twisting lane leads to Hom Green passing Old Hill, a 14th century residence of the Kyrle family. During the reign of Queen Anne, a descendant, Joseph Clarke, built Hill Court, the handsome mansion seen at the end of an impressive avenue of plane trees. In 1888 Hill Court estate was purchased by Major Trafford and remained in his family for nearly 100 years.

Above Walford the path to Spring Herne is lined with a colourful array of wild flowers. Tucked into the slope of Bulls Hill is Wythall, a timber Tudor house occasionally open to the public, said to have been built by William Stratford. Pits, quarries and kilns are remainders of extinct lime and brick making industries on Howle Hill topped by an Iron Age encampment.

From these hills the Wye Valley Walk descends to the pretty hamlet of Coughton with its 'lost' chapel, disused corn mill and former toll cottage lying under Chase Hill alongside Castle Brook. The path steeply climbs Chase Hill to the ramparts of a hill fort covering a cultivated area of 22 acres, its descent skirts Merrivale Wood, now a reserve under the care of the Herefordshire Nature Trust. In 1992 pockets of sycamore were thinned and cherry and ash planted. Many of the trees are covered with ivy, now thought not to harm healthy trees, thick branches of this energetic creeper provide food and shelter for dunnocks, wagtails, chaffinches, blackbird and robins.

A late Victorian reservoir was constructed in Tank Meadow by Thomas Blake M.P. to provide Ross with a pure water supply. From this site emerges a clear view of Ross. The waymarked route meanders from Alton Court through the old town.

Chapter 3

ROSS-ON-WYE *to* HEREFORD

— FACT FILE —

Distance
18 miles (29 km)

Maps
O.S.Landranger sheets 149 and 162

Transport
A regular bus service operates between Ross-on-Wye and Hereford except for a limited service on Sundays. A meagre timetable exists of buses from How Caple, Brockhampton, Fownhope and Mordiford to Hereford. For up-to-date information contact Hereford and Worcester County Council ☎ Worcester 766799.

Parking
Ross-on-Wye, Hole-in-the-Wall, Brinkley Hill, Capler, Mordiford, Hampton Bishop and Hereford.

Picnic Sites
Brinkley Hill, Capler, Swarden Quarry with picnicking permitted along the riverside at Ross-on-Wye, Hole-in-the-Wall and Hereford.

Refreshments
Ross-on-Wye, How Caple, Brockhampton, Fownhope, Mordiford, Hampton Bishop and Hereford.

Accommodation and general visitor information
Tourist Information Centres at :
Ross-on-Wye ☎ 0989 562768
Hereford ☎ 0432 268430

Camp Sites
Wilton, Fownhope, Mordiford and Hereford.
Further information from Tourist Information Centres.

Circular Walks
Waymarked routes can be followed from Ross, Mordiford and there is a nature trail around Lea and Paget's Wood.

The Countryside Service. *This is based at Queenswood Country Park,*
☎ 0568 847052

☞ **ROUTE DIRECTIONS** ☜

At **Wilton Road** car park below **Ross-on-Wye**, a display board and sign directs walkers under the road via a flood arch, over **Banky Meadow** and **Wye Street** to join the riverside path. Follow this to the right passing in front of the **Hope and Anchor Inn**, around the boat house and under the modern **Bridstow Bridge**. The path continues along the riverside for a further ½ mile before bearing right across a field and turning left along a disused railway track lined with a wide variety of vegetation.

Within ½ mile keep an eye out for a sharp right turn down some steps, over a stile and onto a field path rejoining the **Wye** opposite **Backney Common**. The route continues in the same direction through meadows below **Brampton Abbotts** where undefined footpaths lead up to the village with its pretty church. The path skirts young trees at **Monks Grove**, a recently re-planted wood, then proceeds over stiles and through fields to **Foy**. A fork right via a meadow leads to an enclosed grassy track eventually reaching a tarmac lane at **Orchard Cottage**.

Turn left along this lane for nearly 1½ miles following a delightful stretch of the river flowing under **Foy Bridge**, past **Court Farm**, cottages at **Hole-in-the-Wall** and **Lyndor Cottage**. The Wye Valley Walk bears left before the second cattle grid, cross stile into arable fields alongside the river.

Where a brook joins the **Wye**, bear right to the village of **How Caple**. Roads and paths lead to **Kings Caple** and **Hoarwithy**: the way-marked route briefly follows the road to the left before turning beside the old mill. An enclosed bridle-way leads into open fields, where the route is undefined, then bears right to cross a new foot-bridge and ascend to **Totnor**, a delightful little hamlet in the parish of **Brockhampton**.

Follow a tarmac lane to the left over the minor crossroads at **Plastre Tump**, then left along a pleasant track turning right after 500 yards, this leads to a former school and houses at **Ladyridge** and **Brinkley Hill**. Cross the road, follow the track ahead which offers occasional glimpses of the shimmering Wye through dense woods. Pass an isolated cottage on the right before reaching **Capler** with its picnic site and wonderful view of the river below.

Opposite, left of **Capler Lodge**, the **Wye Valley Walk** ascends through woods along a defined track to **Capler Camp**, an Iron Age hill-fort with far reaching views. Turn right along the ramparts and beyond the farm buildings a sharp left turn leads to a flight of steps descending the steep bank of this ancient fortification. A path leads through two fields, bearing left to a farm track leading onto the **Hereford/Fownhope** road.

Turn left along the road, within 200 yards turn right onto another farm track. Before reaching **Overdine Farm**, follow the signed path on the right. It twists and turns through fields to the top of a scenic ridge, then veers left over stiles and through pastures to a stile entering the nature reserve at **Lea** and **Paget's Wood**. In the midst of the reserve fork left and follow a bridle-way to a stile thereby reaching a field-path onto **Common Hill**.

Cross the tarmac lane and follow a path on the righthand side of a cottage, it bears left, then right as indicated by the waymarks. Defunct quarries, now overgrown, are sited before an open area at **Monument Hill**, a small nature reserve with a seat offering splendid views across the river valley. An enclosed track leads to a crossways, follow the bridle-way ahead for about 1 mile passing isolated cottages before descending to the road at **Nupend**. From **Common Hill** a selection of lanes, paths and tracks lead down either to **Fownhope** with its inns, shops and accommodation, or to **Rudge End**, the birthplace of the bareknuckle boxer Tom Spring.

Cross the road and brook at **Nupend** then follow a bridle-way through the fields of a sheltered valley lying between **Haugh Woods** and **Fownhope Park**. After 1½ miles turn left beyond **Hope Springs Farm** to a cluster of dwellings at **Bagpiper's Tump**, bearing right to join a delightful path leading through old orchards to the once busy mill at **Mordiford**. Turn right for a pint at the inn, to explore the village, or follow the **Mordiford Loop Walk**. Otherwise cross the Hereford road and follow a track ahead veering right to rejoin this road, cross the mellow 14th century stone bridge spanning the **River Lugg**.

Turn right over a stile and along a raised flood embankment, savour the tranquil scene of **Mordiford's** church, rectory and riverside, framed by a background of wooded hills. Approaching **Hampton Bishop** turn left along the track to **Rectory Lane**, then turn right past comfortable modern houses mingling with pretty thatched cottages. After a bend in the road, the **Wye Valley Walk** bears right, along a path through a field to the Hereford road and the village inn on the left.

Follow the road to the right for about 150 yards, turn left through

ROSS-ON-WYE *to* FOWNHOPE

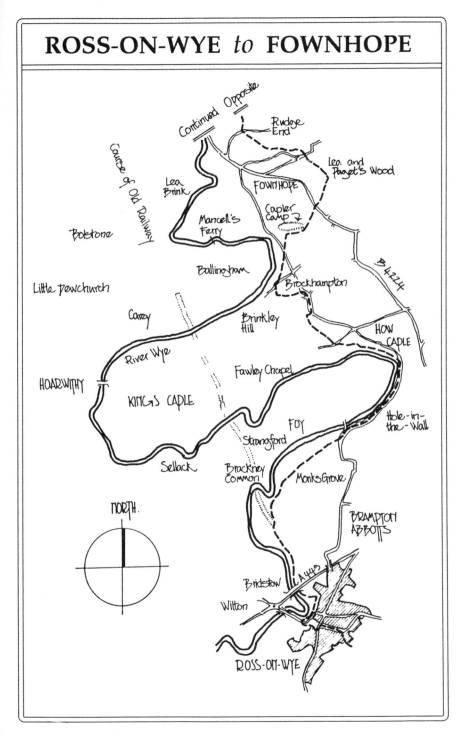

FOWNHOPE *to* HEREFORD

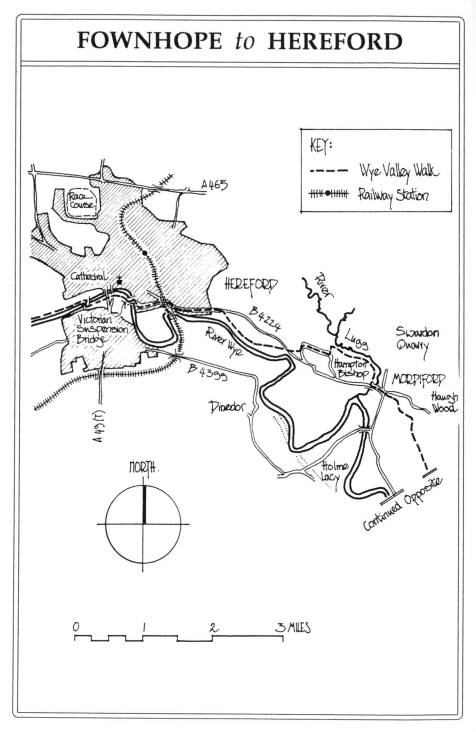

KEY:

– – – Wye Valley Walk

+++●+++ Railway Station

A465

Race Course

Cathedral

HEREFORD

Victorian Suspension Bridge

B 4224

River Wye

River

Lugg

Swardon Quarry

Hampton Bishop

MORPIFORD

B 4399

Haugh Wood

Dinedor

A 49 (T)

Holme Lacy

Continued Opposite

NORTH.

0   1   2   3 MILES

a gate and up steps to the flood embankment and follow the embankment for a short way. A sign directs the route across a field to the Wye, follow an overgrown stretch upstream opposite **Dinedor Hill** and **Rotherwas Chapel**. At **Hampton Park**, near the outskirts of **Hereford**, turn away from the river and cross a stile to rejoin the busy road, turn left to pass an intriguing variety of dwellings: a disappointing entry into the city after the rolling countryside. Once under the railway bridge turn left, follow **Park Road** into **Green Street** and on to **Vicarage Road** past a church, school and footpath to the **Wye**. Turn right alongside the **Wye** bound for the **Victorian footbridge** taking the **Wye Valley Walk** over the river. Continue in the same direction on the opposite bank to the **Wye Bridge**. Otherwise walk across **Bishops Meadow** to the car park at **St Martins Street**. Keep to the east bank through **Castle Green** for **Hereford Cathedral** and town centre.

◆ RURAL HEREFORDSHIRE ◆

Venturing out across the fertile Hereford plain from Ross to Hereford the River Wye runs an exceedingly sinuous 36 mile course, the walker engaged upon the Wye Valley Walk covers half that distance, whilst the humble crow may fly a mere third the distance to the same effect. The walk traverses a comfortable and varied landscape of shy valleys, wooded hills, chattering brooks, charming orchards, fields of cereals, soft fruit or pastures inhabited by cattle, sheep, horses, pigs and poultry. Churches, old and not so old, prominently feature in a satisfying scene dominated by the beautiful Wye, overlooked by ancient hill-forts. The relatively sparce population in this part of the county live in scattered communities linked by winding lanes. Traditionally Herefordshire produced wool, beef, animal hides, dairy produce, wheat, cider, perry, pork, honey and timber. In the 18th century a 500 acre farm would have grown wheat, barley, peas, turnips, mangolds, oats, apples and clover, and reared sheep, cattle, horses and pigs. During the Napoleonic Wars the price of agricultural produce substantially increased, but when peace came in 1815 it was followed by a depression lasting twenty years, the agricultural labourer suffered great hardship and tenant farmers paid excessive rents, tithes, rates and duties. In the 19th century artificial manure and improved implements were introduced, but it was not till the 20th century that any major changes were made in agriculture.

An adjusting economy till the early 1980s forced farmers to merge and enlarge the arable fields, resulting in the removal of hedgerows and woodland which has inevitably had a detrimental effect on wildlife. This is being redressed by new guide-lines in the Wildlife and Countryside Act which go some way to protect these sanctuaries enabling an attractive pattern of fields to remain, sheltered by woods, hedges and coppices. Cattle most often seen on the Wye Valley Walk include Charolais, Fresian, while the world-famous Hereford, with its characteristic white face and 'red' coat, the breed noted for its flavoursome meat, is less suited to the 'lean' culture. Sleek and frisky horses and ponies, now kept for racing, leisure and hunting are often encountered.

For centuries cottagers, smallholders and farmers grew cider apples, but orchards have been depleted in recent years. Farm- and field-names indicate that vineyards once existed, and they have recently been re-introduced with some success. Cheap French wine imported during the 1800s led to a decline in cider consumption, however, at this time cider began to be commercially produced by large companies: this practice continues, with Bulmers of Hereford, as well as on small individual farms. Hops are grown on the eastern side of Herefordshire, and are unlikely to be encountered on the Wye Valley Walk.

The market town of Ross-on-Wye, sits picturesquely between the wooded hills of Chase and Penyard and the River Wye. In Domesday Ross was recorded as a village, with a manor held by the Bishops of Hereford: it was granted a market in the 12th century by King Stephen.

Walkers wishing to explore Ross-on-Wye will need to make a detour from the route. Sites of historical interest are identified by blue plaques, a product of the 1985 Mayor's Project. Ross- on-Wye claims no really dramatic event or famous personages, although several have passed through, including Charles I, Henry IV, Lord Nelson, George IV, Charles Dickens, Alfred Lord Tennyson and Lloyd George.

A few citizens have left their mark on the town, the best known being John Kyrle, 'The Man of Ross', who resided in the half-timbered house opposite the Market House until his death in 1724. Kyrle provided the first water supply, restored the causeway from Wilton, re-built the churchspire and left a walk for future generations to enjoy. In 1786 a certain Walter Scott, who had made his fortune in London as a master plasterer, left money to restore his old school. During Victorian times, James Wallace Richard Hall while working as a solicitor and banker, helped to establish the dispensary, a fore-runner of the Cottage Hospital. He was also involved in founding the British and Foreign School, and the Hereford, Ross, Gloucester

Railway. The monument erected to Hall's memory was dismantled in 1980, making way for a mini roundabout, it was re-erected in 1992 by Ross Civic Society. By the time of Hall's death Thomas Blake had become a prominent businessman, this non-conformist, Liberal M.P. and magistrate improved the town's water supply, re-built the Baptist chapel, and donated a free library, now housing the Tourist Information Centre. He also solved the controversy over access to the Prospect Gardens, which resulted in this magnificent viewpoint being left to the town in perpetuity.

From the 17th century benefactors including William Rudhall, Thomas Webbe, and William Pye built almshouses which still survive as attractive features in the town. Charitable tradition continued into the present century when a group of local men, under the odd name of Larruperz, raised money from their musical performances throughout the 1920s and 1930s to build a community hall. A site was purchased, but the war intervened and the project was delayed, finally, after an exchange of property in 1990 the Larruperz Centre was opened in part of the former Ross Grammar School.

From the Wye Valley Walk a footpath leads from Crossfields to the 13th century church of St Mary the Virgin, an attractive, slender spired, building re-built in 1721 by Kyrle, and again in 1852 after being struck by lightening. Dating back to 1284, St Mary's contains notable features and interesting monuments: a Plague Cross in the graveyard commemorates a disaster which took 315 local lives in 1637, it is interesting to note that Walter Scott's substantial tomb is still maintained by his trust.

The 12th century Bishop's Palace had fallen into ruins by the 16th century. When the site, then occupied by the Pounds Inn, was being prepared by James Barrett in 1837 to erect his Royal Hotel, a curious dungeon, thought to be contemporary with the Palace, was discovered. The hotel was built in the picturesque style to harmonise with the mock Gothic buildings of the 1830s, to wit the red sandstone gazebo tower and town walls, the British and Foreign School, the Lock-up and a Summer House built to replace John Kyrle's original. This active period of development altered the western approach into Ross-on-Wye, establishing the view so much admired today.

The 17th century red sandstone market house stands on the site of the old Booth Hall, in the heart of the town: a constant stream of traffic shakes its crumbling foundations. On Thursdays and Saturdays an array of stalls offer a range a wide range of goods, from locally produced eggs, fruit and cheeses to gaily coloured skirts and scarfs. The livestock market was held here until 1871 when it was moved near the railway where it remained until the late 1980s when it was transferred to a larger site convenient for the motorway.

The wide and curving Broad Street drops down to Brookend, the site of the old Alton Court Brewery demolished in 1992: the former Town Mill re-built in 1857 now houses an antiques business. Beyond this are the Brookend Tanyard and Malt House the former was in use from the 17th century until 1836 when the tanyard ceased operations: the malt house was remodelled as an inn, and eventually closed in the 1960s.

In 1670 the tan-yard was owned by John Merrick the Elder, probably a relative of James Merrick, tanner and quaker, associated with the building in 1667 of the Friends Meeting House in Brampton Street. Within its secluded burial ground rest two respected Quakers, Nathaniel Morgan, a 19th century banker and Henry Southall, a draper who died in 1916.

Ross-on-Wye has held a fascination for scribes. The Hon John Byng, whose tour through South Wales took him through Ross in 1787; Pope, in his Moral Essays, penned the famous poem to John Kyrle in 1732; Coleridge who stayed at the Kings Arms in 1784 and also felt compelled to put pen to paper the 'Man of Ross'. In the summer of 1807 while researching his long poem Robert Bloomfield stayed at the Swan, and Charles Dickens met his biographer John Foster at the Royal in 1867, an event commemorated by a copper plaque in the foyer. The only female writer of note associated with the town, Magiad Evans, lived in and around Ross in the 1930s and 1940s, her writings showed unfulfilled promise before her untimely death in 1958.

From Ross the Wye Valley Walk follows the river from Wilton Bridge, a fine stone arched structure of 1597 replacing an earlier timber version and an unpredictable ferry. The bridge has undergone extensive repairs over the centuries with the latest widening and strengthening scheme completed in 1993. The 13th century castle, now in ruins, was built to defend this important river crossing, the path skirting its overgrown moat affords a closer view. The river must have presented a busy scene during the 18th and 19th centuries with barges up to 65 tons hauling cider, hops, oak bark, wheat and timber from the quay and dock at Wilton and Ross. Pleasure boats plied the river, on the banks, ropes, baskets and boats were made. The Hope and Anchor Inn, and a motor vessel are reminders of such activity and indeed of the popular Wye Tour.

Between Ross-on-Wye and Backney there is a wealth of wildlife, with ducks, swans and signets gliding among waving reeds and under overhanging willows, whilst buzzards, finches, yellow hammers, jackdaws and sand martins haunt this quiet meander. Heron may be spied stalking their prey. In the summer sun dragonflies hover over drifts of white blossomed water crowfoot, frequenting gravel river-beds or the stony remains of bridges, weirs and fords. In July the energetic Himalayan Balsam flowers, its sickly scent easily recognised. Introduced into this country in 1910 it spread rapidly reaching Herefordshire in 1937.

In 1855 the Hereford, Ross, Gloucester Railway opened amidst great celebration. The route between Ross and Hereford crossed the Wye three times, at Backney, Strangford and Carey. When it closed in 1964 the bridges were dismantled, leaving gaunt stone piers. Before sighting the remnants of Backney Bridge, the Wye Valley Walk follows a section of the railway track with its overgrown embankments garlanded with tinted dog roses, brambles, old man's beard and hawthorn. In summer pink and white bunches of campion blend with purple mallow, giant hogweed and yellow vetch.

The surrounding fields grow sugar beet, wheat, barley, potatoes, oilseed rape and sprouts, occasional clumps of poppies struggle to show their cheery red faces. Fields full of grunting pigs add to the interest. The only unwelcome intrusion is the low flying aircraft screaming through this wonderful area.

In 1986 volunteers from the Wye Valley Countryside Service replanted Monks Grove with rows of oak, ash, lime, chestnut, cherry, alder and hornbeam, now well established these trees cover an undergrowth of foxglove, campion and bracken.

Opposite Backney Common, on the east bank of the Wye, a simple metal cross bears the letters H.E, commemorating the Rev Harry St Helier Evans' act of bravery. In 1904 the reverend aged 47, rector of Brampton Abbotts, met his death, whilst saving his son and his daughter's friend.

Above the river an ancient road winds its way from Ross to Brampton Abbotts, Hole-in-the-Wall and How Caple. Considered important enough to be turnpiked by the Ross Trust in 1749 it was abandoned in 1815 and the toll gate at Townsend removed, leading to the establishment of a toll free entry into Ross, much appreciated by farmers and drovers taking their livestock to Ross Market. The road remains an attractive route to Brampton Abbotts with its red brick, former rectory and 12th century church. St Michael's has a timber bell turret, a 14th century porch and a rare early 16th century brass, a memorial to Joan Rudhall from the nearby mansion. The church boasts a novel gadget, restored in 1908, to lift the lid from the font. A water colour painting from 1890 depicts the church after its restoration in 1857, it was further restored in 1907. Wall plaque commemorate rectors which include the unfortunate Harry St Helier Evans.

A generous sweep of the Wye encircles and intersects the parish of Foy, joined by an elegant suspension bridge, replacing the earlier 1876 structure, swept away by floods in 1919. Foy's history is yet to be traced from its 'L' shaped earthwork, Saxon dyke and unidentified castle site. Nothing of Eaton Tregoes castle is visibl today, but in the 19th century remains were recorded at Hole-in-the-Wall. From the 15th to 17th century the castle belonged to the Abrahall family who married into other families including the Walwyns, Kyrles and Hoskyns. In 1673 on the death of the last heir the property was divided then fell into decay.

Other estates in Foy include Inglestone, also owned by the Abrahalls. The original 1616 red brick building was re-built in the mid 1800s. Perrystone was purchased by the Clives in 1865, extended and converted into an attractive mansion. Walkers may care to cross the suspension bridge and follow a riverside path to the delightfully situated church of St Mary founded in the 11th century. Re-built and restored it retains a 14th century porch and tower, a Jacobean pulpit and interesting stained glass windows, monuments of the Abrahalls' dominate the chancel walls and floors.

Where the Wye Valley Walk joins the road at How Caple a right-of-way passes a Norman chapel at Fawley, before continuing to Kings Caple where a pretty church with a 14th century tower and spire provides a prominent landmark. From King Caple another

Footbridge to Foy

suspension bridge leads across the Wye to a remote church at Sellack, alternatively follow twisting lanes to Hoarwithy Bridge, re-built for the second time in 1990. The pretty riverside village of Hoarwithy serves the walker well offering both refreshments and accommodation.

Kings Caple, Sellack and Hoarwithy together with Hentland churches share in the ancient Palm Sunday Pax Cake ceremony, dating back to a charity of 1484. The much photographed Italianate church of St Catherine's in Hoarwithy has featured in at least three films Gaunt and idiosyncratic, with its Tuscan campanile it remains an eccentric part of this village. Designed in 1874 by the prolific London architect John Pollard Seddon, St Catherine's is but one of the many ecclesiastic buildings, houses and schools dotted along the Welsh borders which are memorials to Seddon who acted as Surveyor to the Archdeaconry of Monmouth well into his 74th year. Examples of his work can also be seen in Chepstow, Tintern, Redbrook, Wyesham, Dixton, Goodrich and Hentland.

Accommodation is available at How Caple, and on certain days teas are served at How Caple Court where an Edwardian garden is open to the public. Throughout its long history Caple Court has only been occupied by three families, the Caples, Gregorys and Lees, all of whom have left their mark in the adjoining church which over looks a tranquil, partly wooded, stretch of the Wye. Amongst the scattered tombs is one dedicated to George Prosser, the miller at How Caple, who died in 1847, his wife Margaret continued to run the corn mill until her death in 1855; another headstone relates to the accidental death of 41 year old Charles Hooper at the same mill. The route passes the former mill resting beside Totnor Brook, where remains of its long leat, pond and tail race are still detectable.

New picnic sites at Brinkley Hill and Capler serve as useful parking places either enabling one to join the Wye Valley Walk or follow a riverside route from Brockhampton to Fownhope. Within the grounds of Brockhampton Court Hotel are the ivy draped ruins of the original parish church, replaced in 1901 by one of the prettiest churches on the Wye. Designed by W.R.Lethaby the church epitomises the spirit of the Arts and Crafts Movement, with its thatched roof and mixture of architectural styles: a wild flower theme runs throughout, on the carved choir stalls, embroidered altar cloth, hymn book covers and kneelers. Richly coloured tapestries by Burne-Jones hang on either side of the altar.

From Brockhampton a superb hilly route leads to Fownhope, ascending 600 feet to the double ramparts of Capler Camp, an Iron

Age hill-fort offering brilliant views of the Malverns and Black Mountains. The Woolhope Club excavated the hill-fort in 1923, revealing foundations of a 17th and 18th century cottage and a stone constructed mound. Their finds included a Roman coin, flints, glazed pottery, and fragments of an 18th century wine bottle and clay pipe.

There is a delightful path through Lea and Paget's Wood, now a nature reserve. For centuries these woods have been managed to provide firewood and materials for building, fencing and carpentry. A signed trail leads around the reserve through coppiced hazel, sweet chestnut and wych elm, tall specimens of ash, oak and wild cherry: the rarer small-leaved lime and service trees indicate ancient woodland. Violets, primroses, wood anemones, wild garlic, bluebells and yellow archangel flower in spring followed by orchids, meadow saffron, marsh marigold and dog's mercury. A variety of birds inhabit these woods and dappled fallow deer may be sighted skipping shyly through the trees.

In specific areas throughout the Wye Valley, it is not unusual to catch sight of deer on the edges of wooded hills, herds of up to 50 have been seen peacefully grazing in the lower Wye. There are two species in this area, the familiar fallow, and the Chinese Muntjac, about the size and colour of a fox, timid, secretive and rarely seen. Both 'Common' and 'Black' Fallow deer measure nearly a metre at the shoulder, the former has rich, reddish brown upper parts and the latter has dark upper parts and pale coloured under. Only the male bears antlers which are cast inspring and re-grow by autumn. Fawns are born in May or June and, if found curled up in leaves or long grass, should be left alone as the timid mother is never far away. The fallow has no natural predators except man. Herds are culled to keep numbers in check.

Church Wood has a deep overgrown quarry where limestone was once cut and conveyed to nearby kilns, now partially collapsed and hidden by overgrowth. In the 18th and 19th centuries alternative layers of limestone and fuel were placed in the hole at the top then fired from the furnace below. This produced clinker which fell into the draw hole at the bottom. Slated with water it crumbled into a fine powder which was used as fertiliser and for building. The top of lime kilns were favourite places for tramps to spend a warm and comfortable night. The most famous people associated with lime burners were John Clare, the nature poet and William Turner who depicted them in his paintings.

Overlooking Fownhope the wooded slopes of Common Hill have a network of paths and tracks connecting isolated cottages and old quarries. The hill, once common land, was enclosed by the early

19th century. With a decline in lime production, cider houses closed their doors: The Orange Tree Inn is now a pleasant cottage, while the tumbling remains of the Thatched Tavern provides a habitat for insects, birds and mammals in the corner of a small reserve belonging to the Hereford Nature Trust.

On a sunny day Monument Hill is a wonderful place to study butterflies; hairstreaks, marbled whites, fritillaries and skippers attracted to the lime-loving plants. Fownhope is a conveniently appointed village, well catered for in the way of shops and inns with a post office, school, handsome church and new village hall. Although its former glory as a self-sufficient place is long gone, its former breweries, inns, cider houses, corn mills, hopyards, barkhouses and tan-yard are well documented. During the 19th century there was a rich assortment of tradespeople, including carpenters, wheelwrights, blacksmiths, masons, saddlers, drapes and shopkeepers. The River Wye provided employment for boat builders, salmon fishermen and ferry-men, eight ford or ferry crossings over the Wye are recorded in Fownhope parish; below Capler, at Rocks or Mancell's ferry, the end of Ferry Lane, beside Mill Farm, at Lechmere Ley, opposite Shipley, and at Even Pits where the ferry was replaced in 1858 by Holme Lacey Bridge, re-built in 1973.

The expanding village nestles between the Wye and wooded hills. Former residents are remembered on memorial tablets and headstones in St Mary's Church. Partly Norman, it was restored in 1882 when the minstrels' gallery was removed: 17th and 18th century fonts were unearthed and reinstated; the beautifully carved 12th century tympanum was moved from an outside doorway to its present protected site on the west wall. Capped with an unusual broach spire, the central tower concealed an ancient chest which was there for two hundred years before being hauled down in 1974. The parish stocks and an early 20th century milestone are in evidence outside the building.

Undoubtedly the most famous Fownhope 'citizen' was Thomas Winter, who under a sunnier name, Spring, achieved lasting fame when he became English Bareknuckle Champion in 1823. Tom, a strong lad handy with his fists, was spotted by boxers on a sparring tour and advised to try his luck in London. There,under the tutelage of champion Tom Cribb, Spring became one of the most skilful boxers of the Regency era, rubbing shoulders with artists, writers and even royalty. Legend has it that Tom Spring was landlord of the Green Man Inn at Fownhope, but this is unlikely, however, he did come back to his native county to manage the Boothall Inn at Hereford, before returning to London to take over the Castle Tavern, Holborn, a famous boxing pub, where he died in 1851.

Footpaths lead from Fownhope across fields to the riverside at Lea Brink, where hedges hug an idyllically sited cottage above the Wye as it twists past on its way to Ross. So sheltered and favoured is this warm bank that an eclectic display of wild flowers crowd together: the blues, yellows, pinks and purples of tansy, yarrow, loosestrife, vetch, willow herb, water mint, dog daisy, knapweed and mudwort, all attract bees and butterflies reflecting their rainbow colours in the clear waters of the Wye. In the river, fish slide from under mossy rocks and flowering water crowfoot, while squadrons of shining blue damselflies and dragonflies hover in the heat of a July day.

On approaching Mordiford the Wye Valley Walk passes close to a now semi-derelict building used for the milling of corn and animal feeds, until 1935. The iron water-wheel lies rusty and abandoned, but there are signs of restoration. The prominently positioned Moon Inn has served travellers en route from Hereford to Gloucester for many centuries. The route was turnpiked by the Gloucester and Hereford Turnpike Trust in 1726, taken over in 1730 by the Hereford Trust until the abolition of tolls in 1870: tolls were collected at Castle End, Crow Hill, Old Gore, Mordiford and St Owen's Gate.

Between Fownhope and Mordiford the modern bridge leads over the Wye to Holme Lacey, and Holme Lacey House, one of Herefordshire's largest mansions, whose role in the oncoming 21st century is uncertain. Built by the Scudamores in the 17th century it stands midst extensive parkland overlooking the river. A quiet lane leads to the isolated St Cuthbert's Church housing the effigies and tombs of the Scudamore family who owned the estates here from the 14th century when they succeeded the de Laceys, reflected in the place-name.

Vulnerably sited between the rivers Lugg and Wye, Mordiford is afforded protection by the Stank, a specially constructed embankment. With its cottages, Georgian Rectory and attractive church, the village provides a postcard scene from the parapets of the 14th century bridge and 16th century causeway across the Lugg. The Norman church has undergone changes, mainly in the early 19th century when the present tower replaced a central one which was decorated with a curious painting of a green dragon with red mouth and tongue. Many tales surrounded this fearsome man-eating monster allegedly living in Haugh Woods, and eventually slain by a boy from within a barrel!

To explore this delightful area, follow the waymarked 'Mordiford

Loop Walk', leading through interesting scenery to Backbury Hill, Checkley and Haugh Woods. Alternatively, follow the Wye Valley Walk along the Lugg, cross the river via an intriguing packhorse bridge in the water meadows. Little is known about this crossing, referred to as Hampton Bridge when repairs were reported in the 1742 and 1756 Quarter Sessions.

At Longworth a more recent bridge spans the Frome beside a disused mill. With a gradual ascent to Old Sufton, home for many centuries of the Hereford family who restored the house with its quaint 18th century dovecote. Towards the end of 1700 they built Sufton Court, a more imposing building, which is occasionally opened to the public. A bridle-way leads to Swarden Quarry car park and picnic site also on the Mordiford Loop Walk.

The countryside around Mordiford is exceptional with wooded hills, orchards, pastures grazed by milking herds, fields of hay, oilseed rape or hops, lanes lined with scented honeysuckle, vetch and tangled roses. Following the Stank to Hampton Bishop a different scene emerges, as the Lugg meanders past willows and water meadows. At Hampton Bishop an unsigned footpath leads alongside the former Rectory to St Andrew's Church, another Norman foundation with a distinctive timber-framed tower. Hampton Bishop is a bend of 20th century houses amid attractive 16th and 17th century buildings: the 'Bunch of Carrots', the village inn, takes its unusual name from an 'exclusive' Salmon pool in the nearby Wye.

From the Bunch of Carrots the Wye Valley Walk follows a pleasant riverside path, where a colourful assortment of flowering plants thrive in lush meadows. On the opposite bank, at 600 feet stands Dinedor's Iron Age hill-fort. Occupied between 300 B.C. and A.D. 100, its ramparts now covered with beautiful mature beech trees enclose an area of 12 acres. Sheltered by this hill lies Rotherwas with its chapel, a reminder of a large mansion demolished earlier this century, both these sites are listed as Ancient Monuments and are open to the public.

On the outskirts of Hereford at Hampton Park, the road passes a variety of properties, the 'Vineyard', built on a site reputed to have been the Bishops Vineyard in the 13th century. The road continues under Eign railway bridge, constructed in 1853 to carry the line from Shrewsbury to Newport, an important link from South Wales to the North of England. After Bartonsham the Wye Valley Walk returns to the Wye, crossed by the Victorian Suspension Bridge, opened 'with great ceremony' in 1898, proceed westward to conclude the section at Wye Bridge, with its famous view to Hereford Cathedral.

Chapter 4

HEREFORD to HAY-ON-WYE

— FACT FILE —

Distance
24 miles (38.6 km)

Maps
O.S.Landranger sheets 148 and 149

Transport
A regular bus service operates between Hereford and Hay-on-Wye, with occasional buses to Bredwardine from both places. For further information ☎ *0432 356201 or 352200.*

Parking
Hereford, Breinton Spring and Hay-on-Wye, with unofficial parking possible at Byford, Bredwardine and Clifford.

Picnic Sites
At present non-existent.

Refreshments
Hereford, Belmont, Swainshill, Staunton-on-Wye, Bredwardine, Merbach, Hardwicke and Hay-on-Wye.

Accommodation and general visitor information
Tourist Information Centres at:
Hereford ☎ *0432 268430*
Hay-on-Wye ☎ *0497 820144*

Camp Sites
Hereford, Whitney, Clifford and Hay-on-Wye.

Circular Walks
Breinton, Monnington & Bredwardine (un-waymarked)
***The Countryside Service** is based at Queenswood Country Park, Dinmore*
☎ *0568 847052*

Public Toilets
At Hereford and Hay-on-Wye.

Hereford Cathedral & the old Wye Bridge.

☞ ROUTE DIRECTIONS ☜

From **Hereford's** 15th century **Wye Bridge** the **Wye Valley Walk** keeps to a path on the south bank of the river till crossing the **Wye** over a disused railway bridge at **Hunderton**. It continues along a riverside path below **Broomy Hill Waterworks Museum**, through meadows and over stiles for 1½ miles to **Breinton** with its spring, church and moated site.

Pass the National Trust car park at **Breinton Spring**, continue ahead to a swing-gate on the left, where the path diagonally crosses a paddock to another swing-gate. Cross the tarmac lane and follow a gravel drive to the swing-gate on the left. Keep to the left hand hedge through fields to the road at **Upper Breinton**. Turn right along the road to and beyond a junction as if bound for **Stretton Sugwas**. Shortly a bridle-way on the left winds its way uphill along an enclosed track to a gate. Keep straight ahead through the fields to reach another track, turn left and descend to the road at **Breinton Common** followed to the right.

HEREFORD *to* MONNINGTON

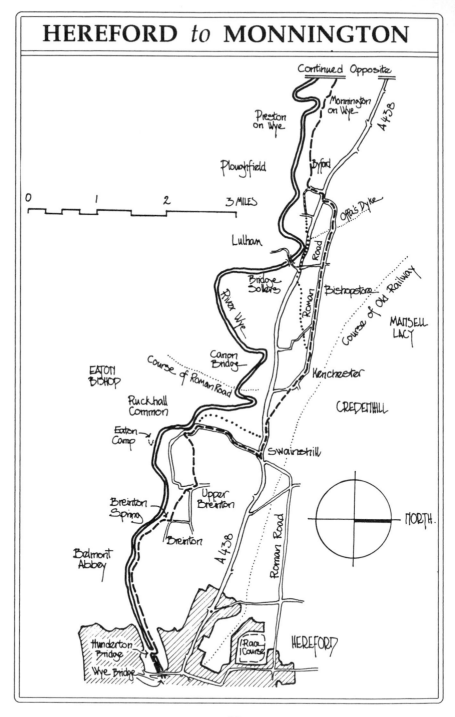

MONNINGTON *to* HAY-ON-WAY

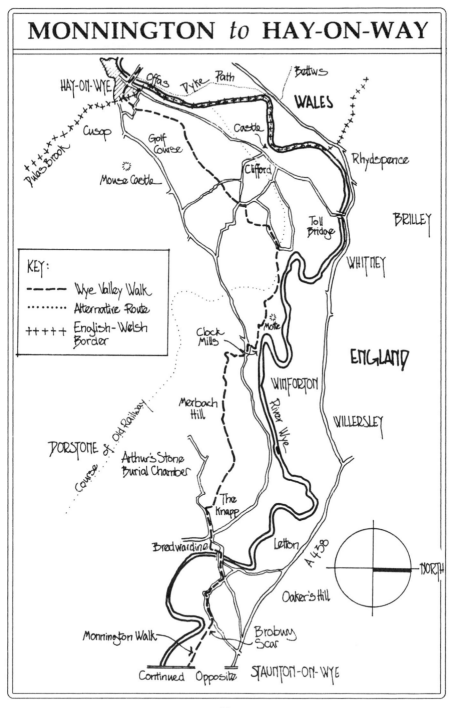

HAY-ON-WYE · Offas Dyke Path · Bettws · WALES

Cusop · Golf Course · Castle · Rhydspence · BRILLEY

Pulas Brook · Mouse Castle · Clifford

Toll Bridge · WHITNEY

KEY:
- – – – Wye Valley Walk
- · · · · Alternative Route
- ++++ English-Welsh Border

Clock Mills · Motte · ENGLAND

WINFORTON · WILLERSLEY

Merbach Hill · River Wye

DORSTONE · of Old Railway

Arthur's Stone Burial Chamber

Course

The Knapp

Bredwardine · Letton · A438 · NORTH

Oaker's Hill

Monnington Walk · Brobury Scar

Continued Opposite · STAUNTON-ON-WYE

61

This is the beginning of an unsatisfactory stretch along tarmac lanes and roads. After the former **Boat Inn** at **Sugwas Passage** the lane bears right to make a pleasant ascent past **Sugwas Court** and **Farm**. On meeting the main **Hereford** road turn left, follow it past the **Kite's Nest Inn**. Fork right along a track between houses and cottages, which winds around before proceeding along the right hand side of fields to arrive at **Kenchester**, follow the tarmac lane to the right.

Ignoring the turn to Credenhill, continue along the lane forming the boundary of **Magnis**, a Roman Town. Pass **Lady Southampton's Chapel**, and follow the course of a Roman road over a distance of 2 miles to **Garnons**, an impressive mansion. The lane bears left to rejoin the main road, thankfully, this is only followed for a few hundred yards. Take a lane on the left leading to **Byford Church**.

An alternative shorter and altogether pleasanter route can be followed from **Breinton Common**, from where the tarmac lane bears right, keep ahead over a stile. Proceed diagonally right across a riverside meadow to another stile. Continue across a series of fields keeping to the right of the **Wye** and **Cliff Covert** till reaching the main **Hereford** road at **Swainshill**. Turn left past the **Kite's Nest Inn** forking right along a track between houses and cottages. This path winds round before proceeding along the right handside of fields to arrive at a tarmac lane. Follow the lane to the right for less than 1 mile through **Kenchester**.

Cross a stile on the left with a footpath sign, then walk diagonally right across fields, over stiles and a tarmac lane. The path continues ahead through fields rejoining the main road at **Bridge Sollers**. Turn right along the road for a ¼ mile, bear left following a signed bridle-way. This heads diagonally right across fields to a metalled lane leading above the **Wye** to meet the **Wye Valley Walk** at **Byford**.

Beyond **Byford Church** follow a waymarked bridle-way on the right leading through a succession of fields to a bridge crossing the **Middle Brook**. The path proceeds through apple orchards to the banks of the **Wye**, bear right following the river for about 200 yards. As the **Wye** meanders away to the left, keep ahead through rows of apple trees to the delightful church at **Monnington**.

Keeping right of the church go through a lych-gate to follow a pleasant grassy path to the tarmac lane. Turn left over a cattle grid then right to stroll through **Monnington Walk**, a beautiful avenue of trees. Proceed through a gate on the right and alongside **Monnington Coppice** to an enclosed track leading to a lovely scenic view of the **Wye** from **Brobury Scar**.

Turn left along a metalled lane, bearing right at the junction, proceed to the cross-roads. Go left past **Brobury House** and over the river via **Bredwardine's** fine six- arched bridge, immediately left a path crosses pastures to Kilvert's church and vicarage.

From the church follow the drive towards the village, a left turn leads to the cross-roads and the **Red Lion Inn.** Ahead a steep climb ascends **Bredwardine Hill.** When the road begins to curve, turn sharp right down a track passing a renovated cottage. Shortly after this, bear left through fields along an undefined path below **The Knapp,** a tree-topped hill. On reaching woodlands, cross the cattle grid and follow the clear track ahead.

After **Woola Farm** bear left along a track leading to a corrugated iron barn, then ahead through level fields to **Merbach Hill** covered in bracken and gorse. A well defined path climbs to over 1,000 feet, offering fantastic views of the **Wye** below. Descend via a steep zig-zag route above an overgrown sunken lane.

Turn right along a path passing a signpost to **Middlewood,** and a modern barn keep ahead before reaching the main **Hay-on-Wye** road. The inn at **Merbach** is on the right. Follow the road left towards **Hay-on-Wye,** turn right along a bridle- way: on the right is a pretty bridge at **Clock Mills,** the path bears left to a stile. Go left through arable fields keeping an ancient hedge on the right until reaching a lane at **Old Castleton.**

Follow this to the right past the remains of a motte and bailey, before **Upper Castleton Farm** turn right along an undefined bridle-path cross the field offering a spectacular view of the **Wye.** The bridle-path gradually descends to the riverside, via a gate leading into a charming wood. From the edge of the wood follow a permissive route going left, then right below a disused railway track. Join and follow the track to the stone bridge, bear left up a slope and keep left along a lane past **The Farm** to **Poolpardon Cottage.** Opposite the cottage a signed path leads straight across fields to a tarmac lane at **Priory Wood.** Cross the lane, follow a short track, turn right along another metalled lane passing a converted barn and restored cottage. Before **Priory Wood Chapel** bear left across the recreation ground, turning left along the lane to a cross-ways.

Keep ahead through a narrow gate, along a path and over a stile, then across fields glimpsing **Clifford Church** on the right. The path joins a track leading to a cattle grid near **Priory Farm,** the site of a 12th century Cluanic Priory. Follow a road left for a few yards to the stile on the right. A pleasant path leads above the delightful **Hardwicke Brook,** crossed via a footbridge beside the ford, continue onto a golf course. The **Wye Valley Walk** is directed to the right, then bears left across the course to a stile leading into fields. Keep ahead towards an avenue of oaks, which is followed to the right. Within a few paces turn left over a stile, a field-path leads to the right of a small wood, through pastures towards **Hay-on-Wye** seen in the distance.

Beside the bungalow cross a tarmac lane to a stile. The path leads straight ahead to **Hay** through a small field, over a sunken brook across another field to a bridge crossing the **Dulas Brook** to **Black Lion Green, Lion Street,** then into **Hay- on-Wye**

◆ KILVERT COUNTRY ◆

From Hereford to Hay-on-Wye there is an opportunity to explore a stretch of undulating countryside which delighted Rev. Robert Francis Kilvert, a Victorian parson reknowned for his diaries, an enduring account of people and places visited in the 1870s. Born in 1840, Kilvert served as a curate at Clyro between 1865 and 1872. He returned to his native Wiltshire, but came back to the Welsh Borders as vicar at Bredwardine from 1877-79, and tragically died only a month after marrying. Since the posthumous publication of his diaries in 1939 the places he so vividly described have become a mecca for literary pilgrims. Sadly much of his original work was destroyed, but the surviving three volumes of his diary accurately record life in Victorian times.

The Wye Valley Walk passes many of the attractive features described by Kilvert, the Monnington Walk, Brobury church, Bredwardine Bridge, Moccas Park, Rhydspence Inn, Hay Castle and Clifford Priory. On foot he covered considerable distances; he also travelled in a gig, and occasionally by train using the Hereford to Hay line which opened in 1864. Today's visitors are reminded of Kilvert's years at Clyro where his former vicarage is now an art gallery named after him. A simple white cross marks his grave at Bredwardine, and a stone seat to his memory stands under a yew: in 1948 the Kilvert Society was formed to promote interest in his life and work.

Hereford poets whose names survive include John Davies, active in the mid 16th century, Thomas Trehern, rector of Credenhill in the 1650s, and John Phillips, buried at the cathedral in 1708, and remembered for a lengthy poem about cider.

The landscape around the City inspired artists, James Wathem, Cornelius Varley, David Cox and Brian Hatton, the latter's work may be viewed at Churchill Gardens Museum. The stage was represented by Roger Kemble, his daughter Sarah Siddons, and David Garrick who trod the boards during the 17th and 18th centuries. Nell Gwynne, Charles II's mistress was born in Pipewell Lane, now called Gwynne Street, a plaque commemorates her birthplace. Early 18th century musical evenings led to the establishment of the Three Choirs festival which still takes place annually either at Hereford, Gloucester or Worcester: many well known local composers have been associated with this event including Edward Elgar, who lived in Hereford for several years, Gustav Holst from Cheltenham, Herbert Howells from Lydney, Rutland Boughton who resided at Kilcot and Vaughan Williams and Frederick Delius from Gloucestershire.

In Kilvert's time the population of Hereford was 15,000. It was a bustling self-sufficient place with good communications by road, rail and canal. There was an excellent livestock and produce market in a city described at the time as clean and well paved with spacious and handsome public buildings. These included a Shire Hall, County Hall where concerts were regularly held, Corn Exchange, Workhouse, Library, Public Baths, Gas Works, a Theatre and a Gaol. Many of these buildings have now been demolished or put to other uses.

Hereford, 'ford of the army', originated in Saxon times, developing around an ancient river crossing. The early town with its cathedral and monastery was encircled by a defensive wall. Although the Normans built a castle in 1055 Welsh invaders destroyed it, the city and the cathedral. Consequently Hereford's defences were reinforced and extended enclosing a reconstructed castle, re-built cathedral and market place. The city became an important trading centre protected by its strong walls, which withstood several Civil War sieges. Towards the end of the 18th century the castle and walls fell into disuse and the six surviving gate-houses were demolished to improve access. Sections of the Saxon and medieval walls can still be seen, at a landscaped area known as Castle Green, where Hereford's own Nelson's Column was erected in 1809.

Hereford is proud of its cathedral which stands in a prominent position reflecting its glory in the River Wye. Originally founded in 676 the present edifice dates from the 11th century with many later additions including the 13th century Lady Chapel, and 15th century Vicars Cloister. Amongst the Cathedral's most precious possession is the Mappa Mundi, a circular world map of 1289, which until more recent times had hung in the Cathedral barely noticed by visitors: on recognition of its true value it has been displayed more securely as part of a permanent exhibition. This wonderful treasure was the centre of national debate during the early 1990s with the possibility of its sale to pay for the Cathedral upkeep. The Cathedral also houses a medieval chained library containing over 1400 books and 227 manuscripts, spanning the 8th to 15th centuries. The Diocesan Treasury displays many valuable items of interest. In the north transept is the tomb of St Thomas Cantilupe, a late 13th century bishop, whose relics are associated with miraculous cures.

Adjoining the cathedral is the Bishop's Palace with its great hall and garden sloping to the banks of the Wye. Other ecclesiastical buildings of note are the churches of St Peter and All Saints. The latter has a leaning spire, ornate pulpit, carved misericords, breadshelf and chained library. St Peter's was comprehensively restored in the late 19th century. Opposite the Cathedral is the City Library, Museum and Art Gallery built during Victoria's reign. From the Cathedral Close Church Street leads to High Town and its 17th century Old House, the only survivor of a line of buildings known as Butcher's Row. An enclosed Butter Market sells fresh and local produce, but before 1862 a magnificent 16th century Market Hall stood at the centre of High Town, its position now marked by a few red stones. The present 1904 Town Hall stands nearly opposite the impressive Shire Hall built in 1819 by Sir Robert Smirke who also designed the British Museum.

The Tourist Information Centre, located in King Street, offers an assortment of leaflets describe the city's history and pin-point buildings and sites of particular interest.

From earliest times Hereford offered bed and board to travellers in modest ale and cider houses which later became coaching inns. In 1774, after improvements to roads by the Turnpike Trusts a coach service to London was established, although the Swan and Falcon, New Inn and Redstreak Tree were used as coaching inns, it was the Green Dragon that came into prominence, it still operates as a hotel.

Wine and spirits were purchased from merchants who shipped wine from France, Spain and Portugal, and ran their own distilleries. Pulling and Co. began trading at East Street in 1813: its former bond warehouse has been carefully converted into dwellings known as Pullings Mews. Beer and cider have been made locally for centuries, and although hops are still grown in the county no major brewer remains. Production of cider, which became the traditional beverage, is dominated by Bulmers who started over 100 years ago. The Cider Museum, reveals the history of cider making, with displays from farm to factory production. In Victorian Hereford various breweries existed in the city including the Hereford Brewery founded in 1834 which grew and expanded: after changes of ownership and takeovers it eventually became a bottling plant and was demolished in the early 1960s. A supermarket now occupies this site. The former Dorset Ale Store, an attractive stone built warehouse beside the Wye, is further evidence of this trade.

From 1858 the Hereford Brewery was run by the father of Alfred Watkins, a notable Herefordian born in 1855. While working for the brewery Watkins travelled around the county he grew to know and love. This was reflected in his life-long interest in archaeology and local history. During a full life he became an inventor, magistrate, county councillor and politician, but is mainly remembered for his radical theories on 'ley lines', expounding a rationale that natural landmarks were used by prehistoric man to establish track-ways. Watkins left a wealth of visual and written material about Herefordshire, ley lines, bee keeping an photography which can be studied at Hereford Library and Record Office.

The City of Hereford was involved with the woollen, timber, brick, tile, livestock and tanning industries. Oak bark was readily available for the three tanyards that, produced leather for harness and shoes: a photograph, taken in 1896 at the Barton Tanyard, showing workmen with their tools of trade is exhibited at Hereford Museum. Earlier industrialised activities have, in modern times, expanded with the emergence of light engineering, plastic moulding, poultry and dairy production. As well as by road, goods were conveyed to and from Hereford on the Wye. In 1662 an effort was made to establish the river as a commercial waterway, but this and later schemes were unable to cope with unpredictable water levels and rapid currents. The Hereford and Gloucester Canal was late to arrive at Hereford, in 1845, only eight years before the opening of the first railway, although a tramway to Abergavenny had been in operation from 1829 to 1853. An extended network of trains soon took trade away from the river which is now exclusively used for recreational purposes. The canal has deteriorated but some stretches are being preserved by a local society. A recent arrival at Greyfriars is the Wye Invader, a barge which, in 1989, navigated 75 difficult miles from Chepstow, and consent is being sought to convert the Dutch barge into a floating restaurant.

While following the Wye Valley Walk through Hereford a variety of river crossings are identifiable. Bartonsham Boat which operated in the 1930s, the elegant Victorian suspension bridge of 1898, the site of the original ancient ford, the Wye Bridge built in 1490 replacing a former 12th century timber structure, the modern Greyfriars Bridge constructed in the mid 1960s, an iron railway bridge at Hunderton used between 1853 and 1966, and the site of the Hunderton ferry which plied the river during the first half of this century. A water tower stands above a Victorian Pumping Station, now housing the Broomy Hill Waterworks Museum. Beyond this, the Wyeside path leaves the city to re-enter a rural landscape.

Yellow Iris.

The riverside path from Broomy Hill is frequently used by joggers, fishermen, dog walkers and ramblers. Despite this the river attracts coots, mallards, cormorants, swans and the occasional kingfisher. The unpleasant aroma of Himalayan Balsam lingers into the late autumn, otherwise the riverside hedgerows are a painter's palette of golds, reds and yellows with pink spindle-berries peeping through. Within one mile of Hereford, the landscape is attractively undulating passing below Belmont House which stands on the opposite bank. Built in 1790 with Victorian additions the mansion was the home of the Wegg-Prosser family, who in 1854 commenced building a Roman Catholic church (and late boarding school) nearby, known as Belmont Abbey. Belmont House and grounds have more recently been converted into a hotel and golf course with emerald fairways sweeping down to the Wye.

At Breinton a network of paths and lanes offer a choice of routes around the parish. St Michael's church dates from the 12th century, but was extensively re-built in the 1860s by F.R.Kempson. With its distinctive broach spire surrounded by orchards it makes a pretty picture. Nearby an unobtrusive mound is all that remains of a moated site occupied during the 12th. century. Below it a cool spring tumbles out of the sandstone rock into the river. This never failing supply is bottled today by individuals seeking free, unadulterated drinking water. This interesting area, Breinton Spring, is under the jurisdiction of the National Trust who provided a car park.

At Breinton Common a well preserved mile post is a reminder of a former toll road leading from Hereford to Sugwas Passage, where until the early part of this century a ferry conveyed livestock, vehicles and foot passengers across the river to Lower Eaton. A mellow red brick building with its fading name once served as the Boat Inn, is now a private residence. From here the Wye Valley Walk at present follows unyielding tarmac lanes and sometimes unpleasantly busy roads over a distance of nearly seven miles, but we have discovered a much more attractive route. The official walk passes the entrance to Sugwas Court re-built in 1792 on the foundations of a Bishop's Palace, visited by Thomas Cantilupe during the 13th century. An abandoned road leads directly to Hereford along a route still partly preserved as a right-of-way.

Stretton Sugwas and Kenchester lie along the course of a Roman road below the wooded slopes of Credenhill, the site of an Iron Age hill-fort. The Romans built a walled town at Kenchester called Magnis or Magna Castra. Numerous excavations have discovered massive defences, substantial buildings and a pattern of roads, what now remains is an unimpressive kite shaped pasture enclosed by hedges. A pleasant detour to explore Magnis follows a footpath across this historic site to a remaining bridge of the Hereford, Hay, Brecon Railway which was in use between 1864 and 1962, then through fields, and along a lane to Kenchester church; a secluded Norman building in which a column, believed to be Roman, has been hollowed out to form a font. The history of Kenchester and its discoveries have been reported at length in books and learned journals. Finds include pottery, mosaic tiles, coins, jewellery and a 3rd century milestone which are housed at Hereford Museum. Further Roman remains have been discovered at Bishopstone, New Weir Byford and along the routes of Watling and Stone Streets.

At Weir Gardens, the National Trust maintain delightful woodland walks offering fine views, with an opportunity to investigate surviving masonry and a cistern from the Roman period. Before leaving Kenchester a Methodist chapel of 1830 named after Lady Southampton is passed. It stands accompanied by its red brick manse, around the corner from a former schoo now converted into a home. From here walkers follow a stretch of Roman road, which eventually leads into Wales.

At Bishopstone cross-roads the more adventurous can head north to explore the church founded in the 12th century with restorations carried out over the last two centuries. In this building, dedicated to St Lawrence, is a tablet commemorating the Herefordshire naturalist, Humphrey Adam Gilbert, a barrister, cricketer, ornithologist, fisherman and author. Born in 1866 he spent an active life advocating bird protection through his lectures and books. He wrote 'The Tale of a Wye Fisherman' in 1928. In the church are stone effigies of John Berrington and his wife who, in the 17th century, lived at Bishopstone Court. This interesting house stands nearby and is still surrounded by a moat with a 16th century gateway and an 18th century bridge.

A mile and a half from Bishopstone is the pretty village of Mansel Lacy sheltered by the woods of Foxley, an estate owned in the 18th century by Uvedale Price, a leading light in the Picturesque Movement. South of Bishopstone, below Bridge Sollers church, an iron bridge of 1896 spans the Wye. This leads to the Golden Valley and the riverside parishes of Preston-on-Wye, Madley and Eaton Bishop. The Wye Valley Walk keeps to the north bank of the river skirting Garnons, a castellated mansion standing in a magnificent position overlooking parkland landscaped by Humphrey Repton in the 1790s. In its grounds is the continuation of the Roman road, and sections of Offa's Dyke, an earthwork constructed in the 8th century by King Offa to form a boundary between Mercia and Wales. On the busy main road between Bridge Sollers and Byford part of this dyke can still be seen.

Byford church's walls are covered with monuments to the Cotterells from Garnons. Other items of note are the Benefaction Boards, a 14th century wall painting, attractive flower decorated plaques from the 1700s and a font dated 1638. Byford, as the name suggests, was once a fording pace with a ferry. A timber yard, saw pit, dock and wharf existed here before navigation on the Wye ceased after the spread of the railways from the mid 19th century From Byford a bridle-way leads through fields to Monnington where the Rev. Francis Kilvert came to visit his sister, who was married to the vicar here. Today Monnington lies quietly hidden amongst acres of orchards, where different varieties of fruit are specially grown for cider making. A step back in time is imagined on entering St Mary's church, built by Uvedall Tomkyns and his wife in 1679 on the site of an earlier building. Apart from the tower, architecture and fittings are virtually unchanged since its construction. A centuries old tradition associates this church with Owain Glyndwr, the Welsh freedom fighter. It is said that he was buried here in the early 1400s.

Nearby the Monnington Walk, a wonderful wide straight avenue of trees leads from Monnington Court to Brobury Scar. The Scots pines and yews of the Walk were probably planted by one of the Tomkyns in the 17th century. A footpath leads to the water's edge, where Moccas Toll bridge stood from 1868 to 1960 when it was damaged by floods and not restored. Moccas Court is visible on the opposite bank. Designed by Robert Adam the mansion was built in 1783 with grounds laid out by Lancelot 'Capability' Brown. It is occasionally open to the public. Beyond the Court is a deer park where ancient and gnarled oaks stretch to the top of Dorstone Hill.

At Brobury Scar, a sandstone cliff, clothed with beeches, their glorious autumn shades reflected in the river below. Up to the end of the 19th century a ferry from Brobury crossed the Wye to Moccas. The collapsed and overgrown remains of a boat-house lies forgotten beside a sunken bridle-way leading to the river crossing. The lane to Brobury is lined with hedges rich with autumn crops of hips, haws, sloes, nuts and blackberries. The village's redundant church contains a surviving 13th century chancel now converted into a house with a curious modern addition. Brobury Gardens and Gallery provide a pleasant pause to enjoy a selection of watercolours, prints and maps for sale. The Victorian house is surrounded by semi-formal gardens, open during the summer, for visitors to stroll along paths to pools, terraces and viewpoints.

The small village of Bredwardine is widely known, thanks to the Rev.Francis Kilvert's diaries. Bredwardine's earlier history dates from Norman times when a church and castle were built along the banks of the Wye. St Andrew's church retains some Norman work, a re-built 15th century chancel, a 1790 tower and a Victorian roof. In the churchyard as well as Kilvert's grave and memorial seat a large tomb is dedicated to George Jarvis, a local benefactor. In his will of 1793 Jarvis left £30,000 in trust for the poor of Bredwardine, Staunton-on-Wye and Letton to provide for their medical, clothing and schooling needs.

Scanty earthworks and traces of fishponds are all that remain of Bredwardine's castle and a later 17th century building. It is said that stones from the ruins of the castle were used to build the original Moccas Court. The 14th century Old Court still survives standing near an earlier moated site and Bredwardine's handsome 18th century brick built bridge. Several places in the village are associated with Kilvert, the Old Vicarage where he lived before and after his brief marriage, Bredwardine Hall, then known as The Cottage, The Knapp, a distinctive tree-topped hill, the Old School which closed in 1969, and cottages at Crafta Webb which have since disappeared. Merbach Hill stands at over 1,000 feet overlooking a plain where the Wye snakes past Winforton, Willesley and Letton, where constant flooding has always been a problem. From Merbach's bracken clad slopes superb views encompass eleven counties. Disused pits and quarries suggest former industries approached by a network of footpaths and bridle-ways, many sunken with centuries of wear. At the southern end of this scenic ridge is a prehistoric burial tomb, known as Arthur's Stone. This high area is haunted by the buzzard whose mew is easily recognised. Redstarts may be sighted in the summer months.

Clifford, one of the largest parishes in England, nestles between Merbach Hill and the banks of the Wye. At Clock Mills landscaping prevents a view of buildings which operated as a mill from before 1754 and continued up to the 1930s. Millers, Jenkins, Powell, Russell, Harris, Evans, Jones, Lloyd and Edwards also ran a ferry service but today only a public bridle-way fords the Wye to Winforton. At Old Castleton the remains of a motte and bailey are visible, while further west are the eye-catching ruins of Clifford Castle, built above the Wye to defend an ancient ford. The first Baron of Clifford was reputed to be the father of Fair Rosamund, the mistress of Henry II. During Welsh raids

Owain Glyndwr's men damaged the castle in the early 15th century. Two hundred years later the castle lay in ruins.

Interesting remains of railway embankments and bridges can be seen at Clifford. The Hereford, Hay, Brecon line, constructed in 1864, travelled the route of an earlier horse-drawn tramway dating from 1816, a branch line in 1889 was added to Pontrilas in the Golden Valley. Near the ruined castle, below a railway embankment, a gate leads to a nature reserve. Known as Clifford Common, it is not grazed, allowing a variety of water-loving plants to thrive beside the river, with deciduous trees providing a habitat for woodland birds.

As the Wye meanders around Clifford it creates a series of deep salmon pools, large catches have been recorded at Cowpond Pikes and Locksters. Here a swirling stretch of water slides around a broad and sinuous bend. An unsigned footpath from here leads through riverside meadows to Whitney Toll Bridge, which boasts an interesting and well documented history dating from a former ford replaced by a stone bridge in 1773. Strong river currents caused the first three bridges to collapse, so a timber and stone structure was specially designed, which since 1802 has withstood the vagaries of the Wye. The toll bridge leads to Brilley, Whitney-on-Wye and Rhydspence, places visited by Kilvert while a curate at Clyro.

Clifford church is perched on a hill amid a graveyard full of whispering yews, cypresses and Scots pines. Designated as a conservation area, wildlife is preserved amongst tilting rows of weathered tombs. Trees, plants, moths, mosses and lichen are painstakingly recorded and lists are displayed by the lych-gate. Carefully sited nest boxes encourage up to fifty different species of birds. St Mary's dates back to the 13th century with major alterations made during Victoria's reign. It's timber roof and wooden pillars provide an unusual interior, while monuments of note include a wooden effigy of a 13th century priest, marble tablets to the Penoyre family and a plaque to Hubert Bagster Trumper who served his country on land, sea and air, and worked as a family doctor in Hay-on-Wye, who wrote about his experiences in the Welsh Borders.

Within sight of the church are the rambling buildings of Priory Farm occupying the site of a Cluanic Priory founded in the 12th century and demolished during the Dissolution. A Victorian house called The Priory, burnt down in 1930, was visited by

Francis Kilvert in July 1870 to celebrate the eclipse of the moon with cups of iced claret and bowls of strawberries. Also to be found in this area is a Calvanistic Methodist chapel dated 1827 which overlooks a small recreation ground.

Clyro, across the river from Hay, is clearly visible from the stretch between Clifford and Hay-on-Wye. It is dominated by the church in more ways than one, for it was here from 1865 to 1872 that Robert Francis Kilvert served as curate to the Rev. Richard Lister Venables. The Diarist admitted passing the happiest years of his short life at Clyro, administering to his parishioners and walking an area later to become famous as 'Kilvert Country'. He was out in his beloved countryside in all weathers and in the vicious winter of 1870, on St Valentine's Eve the Curate trudged two miles up to Bettws, drawn by the merry tolling of the chapel bell. When he finally battled through the snow and icy wind to reach the cold little chapel Kilvert's beard and moustache were frozen to his face, making it difficult for him to open his mouth. A baby was being baptised and Kilvert reported seeing the infant in the font, swimming around in broken ice and water.

On the final stretch to Hay the Wye Valley Walk follows a pleasant dingle formed by the Hardwicke Brook, which in earlier days drove three watermills. The tower in the distance once belonged to The Moor, home of the Penoyres. Fishponds, lodge gates and a splendid avenue of oak trees are all that remains. A golf course is at present being constructed on former farmland, now denuded of hedges and trees. The entry into Hay-on-Wye is across Potter's Lane and over the Dulas Brook which forms the boundary between *Herefordshire* and *Powys*, England and Wales.

Kingfisher.

Chapter 5

HAY-ON-WYE *to* BUILTH WELLS

--- **FACT FILE** ---

Distance
25 miles (40 km)

Maps
O.S.Landranger sheets 147 and 161

Transport
There is a regular bus service between Hay-on-Wye and Builth Wells serving Llowes, Glasbury, Boughrood and Erwood. Builth Wells Railway Station is served by the Heart of Wales line from Shrewsbury and South Wales. Please ring Powys County Council for further information ☎ 0597 826642/3.

Parking
Hay-on-Wye, Glasbury, Erwood and Builth Wells.

Picnic Sites
Hay-on-Wye, Erwood and beside the Wye at Builth Wells.

Refreshments
Hay-on-Wye and Builth Wells. Wayside inns are found at Llowes, Glasbury, Llyswen and Boughrood, with refreshments seasonally available at Erwood

Accommodation and general visitor information
Tourist Information Centres at:
Hay-on-Wye ☎ 0479 820144
Builth Wells ☎ 0982 553307
Llandrindod Wells ☎ 0597 822600

Camp Sites
Hay-on-Wye, Glasbury, Erwood and Builth Wells.
☎ 0597 822600 for information.

Circular Walks
Can be followed from Hay-on-Wye, Broughrood, Erwood and Builth Wells,

along paths that may or may not be signed.
Rights-of-Way Officer, *Powys County Council, Llandrindod Wells*
☎ *0597 826583.*

Public Telephones
Hay-on-Wye, Glasbury, Llanstephan, Erwood, Crickadarn & Builth Wells.

Public Toilets
Hay-on-Wye, Glasbury and Builth Wells.

☞ ROUTE DIRECTIONS ☜

From **Hay-on-Wye** the **Wye Valley Walk** may be joined from the **Black Lion Inn** in **Lion Street.** Follow a lane alongside the inn towards **The Green,** but take the left fork leading to a stile. The field-path follows the line of the medieval town walls before reaching another stile. Cross **Newport Street** and keep ahead along **Wyeford Road** to the banks of the **Wye,** a left turn leads to **Hay Bridge.**

Cross the bridge and continue up the road for approximately 350 yards to a sign directing left, alongside a field hedge. A stile leads onto **Wyecliff,** a scenic site above the river where snow-drops cover the bare earth in winter. The path bears right through a small wood over a footbridge and left to a solitary cottage, then past a memorial stone dedicated to Bill Barker 1894-1953, proceeding along willow and alder lined river banks for nearly two miles.

Where a field narrows, bear right up steps and over a stile joining a footpath going left below the **Hereford** to **Brecon** road which it joins to **Llowes.** Continue along this for about ½ mile. Behind the **Old School** is the church of **St Meilig** with it's ancient stone font and legendary Celtic cross.

Turn right at the **Radnor Arms** up a tarmac lane. Opposite a row of prize-winning council houses, turn left over a stile and follow an undefined path ascending to a stile into **Bryn-Yr-Hydd Common.** Extensive views of the **Black Mountains** above the meandering **Wye** are savoured from the pleasant woodland path,which winds around in the same direction and joins a track leading through rustic **Brynyrhydd Farm** and turning left rejoin the main road. This is followed right for another ½ mile towards **Glasbury.**

Ignore a road on the right leading up to the beautifully kept old chapel at **Maesyronnen,** and past **Maellwch Castle** (rebuilt), however, the **Wye Valley Walk** goes left at the junction, following a footpath across fields, through swing gates and along the **Wye** to **Glasbury** with its modern bridge, Victorian church, shops, inns and canoe launching site.

Keeping the same side of the river, follow the road from the bridge bearing left through the village to beyond the **Old Forge.** A well defined route on the left leads along the river to **Glasbury Farm,** continue between fields sometimes flooded in winter. The route bears right at a signed fork and passes the remains of **Pwll-y-baw,** where an improved path, now drained, joins a tarmac lane at **Boughrood Brest** where a diversion is planned by **Powys County Council.**

Follow the lane around several bends, then turn left beside **Brest Cottage.** An enclosed muddy track leads onto a field-path and along a wooded cliff-top. Descend steps before a gate to the riverside, where the path continues in the same direction beside rocky pools and flood debris, around the **Old Rectory** sloping up to the road. Turn left and follow this through **Boughrood,** passing the village stores, inn and former toll house. Cross the handsome stone bridge, gracefully spanning the **Wye.**

Once across **Boughrood Bridge,** turn right along a tarmac lane leading between the school and the river. There is an excellent view of both the bridge, and **Boughrood Castle,** re-built as a mansion in the 19th century. An earlier ford or ferry crossing is identifiable before reaching **The Shrubbery** and **Water Works.**

The path becomes grassy, following a delightful stretch of the **Wye.** It passes a standing stone in one of the fields; an enclosed, overgrown graveyard sheltered by gnarled yews; a brook that gurgles and leaps through a pretty dingle; the **Wye** drops impressively over rocky falls, where a pair of goosanders grazed on the white foam, and secluded fishing coves shaded by mature oaks, chestnuts and beech. On the left sits the vast **Llangoed Castle,** re-built at the turn of the century and now a hotel. After passing dwellings at **New Gardens** bear left, alongside **Afon Sgithwen** to the main **Hay** to **Builth** road.

Follow the road past **Trericket Mill,** within 200 yards turn right crossing **Llanstephan** suspension bridge over the **Wye.** Keep to the tarmac crossing the disused railway track, then bear left along a lane, the former course of the **Mid Wales Railway:** the verges are designated a Roadside Nature Reserve. Another diversion

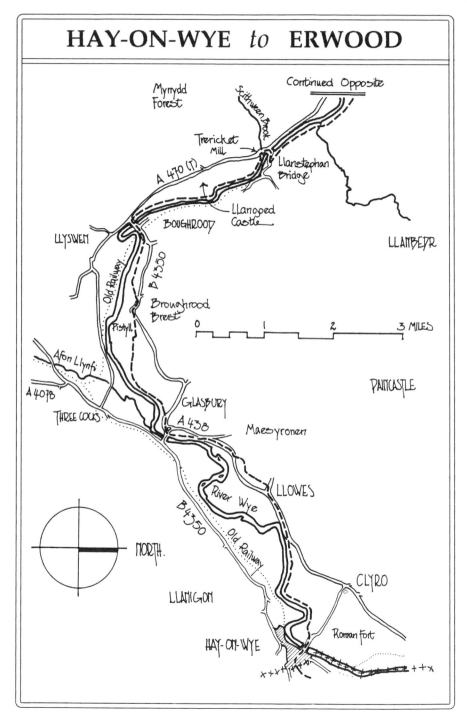

Mynydd Forest

Scithwen Brook

Continued Opposite

Trericket Mill

Llanstephan Bridge

A 470 (T)

LLANBEDR

Llangoed Castle

BOUGHROOD

LLYSWEN

Old Railway

B 4350

Broughrood Breast

0   1   2   3 MILES

Pistyll

PAINCASTLE

Afon Llynfi

A 4078

GLASBURY

THREE COCKS

A 438

Maesyronen

LLOWES

River Wye

B 4350

Old Railway

NORTH.

CLYRO

LLANIGON

Roman Fort

HAY-ON-WYE

ERWOOD *to* BUILTH WELLS

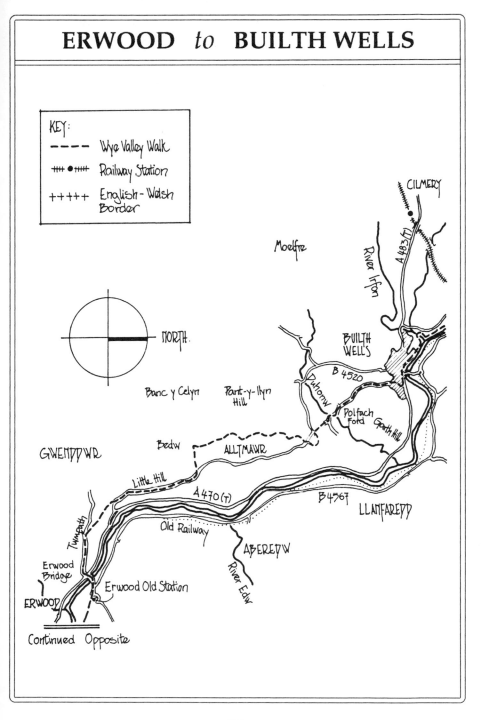

KEY:
- – – – – Wye Valley Walk
- ┼┼┼●┼┼┼ Railway Station
- ┼┼┼┼┼ English – Welsh Border

NORTH.

CILMERY

Moelfre

River Irfon

A483(T)

BUILTH WELLS

B4520

Dulhonw

Polfach Fotd

Goath Hill

Banc y Celyn

Pant-y-llyn Hill

Bedw

ALLTMAWR

GWENDDWR

Little Hill

A470(T)

B4567

LLANFAREDD

Old Railway

Twinpath

ABEREDW

Erwood Bridge

Erwood Old Station

River Edw

ERWOOD

Continued Opposite

maybe implemented along this section. Rising to over 1,000 feet the hills to the right are capped with ancient earthworks.   The lane leads straight to **Erwood Station**, now a craft shop and   tea-room, with parking and picnic site.

From the old station turn sharp left and follow the **Wye Valley Walk** through a swing-gate, down a muddy bank, passing   **Tollgate Cottage** to the road at **Erwood Bridge**. Over the **Wye** follow the tarmac lane ahead to the other side of the main road. Known as the **Twmpath** this was used in the past by drovers.   After a ½ mile climb, turn right along a recently signed route which crosses an open hillside resplendant with mosses, ferns and bracken.   Pursue the remnants of a green lane through fields to a footbridge and ford across the **Fernant**: a delightful cameo featuring cows, sheep, ponies, ducks and hens enjoying the brook and the simple freedom of sloping pastures.

After the footbridge turn right then left, as directed, following a tarmac lane which reveals spectacular views, after the steep zig-zagging ascent over **Little Hill**. At **Brynhaul** the lane veers right along a sheltered, scenic stretch for about a mile, till reaching a junction of lanes and tracks at **Bedw**. This is the start of   an invigorating hill walk: during inclement weather follow an alternative route along the lane for a further 2 miles to **Bedw-fach**.

From the sign on the left at **Bedw** follow a short track to a gate   leading onto the open hills of   **Alltmawr** where the **Wye Valley Walk** rises to 1,400 feet its highest point so far. From the gate continue ahead, bear right to follow a signed bridle-way leading in a northerly direction for 2 miles across bracken clad slopes, over infant streams and brackish pools.   Through swirling mists the scene seems wild and remote, overlooking the distant **Wye** and the **Aberedw Rocks** the site of Llewelyn's Cave. The path descends through a series of gates to **Pantpyllau** and a small farm on the left. The way continues along an enclosed track past a ruined building at **Bedw-fach** to a tarmac lane. The official route crosses this lane, follows a byway ahead bear left, rejoin the same lane. Take an immediate right along a sunken lane, acting as a water course   during the rainy   season, descending to a remote cottage. Cross the **Afon Duhonw** via either ford or footbridge. A tarmac lane leads uphill, around bends, to a junction, follow the lane ahead, which becomes **Newry Road** as it enters **Builth Wells**.

Turn right along **Castle Road**, then left along **Castle Street** to rejoin the **River Wye** at **Builth Wells'** fine arched bridge.

◆ LEGENDARY WALES ◆

Upstream of Hay we enter a landscape steeped in legend, history and folklore. Throughout this section the river either follows a wide, meandering course or gushes through steep rocky valleys. This is a land of enigmatic standing stones; shadowy ruins; wooded mottes; remote churches; hidden caves and ancient river crossings all wrapped in myth and legend.

Stories of Llewelyn's death, Glyndwr's revolts, Macnamara's rakish behaviour and the eccentricities of the Victorian Rev.Price abound. Drovers have left a legacy of inns and roads named after them. Border folklore features witches, wizards, fairies, dragons, ghosts and holy wells, all closely linked with a wild and stunningly beautiful landscape with a strong Christian tradition.

Once across Dulas Brook the Wye Valley Walk enters Powys and skirts around the fascinating border town of Hay-on-Wye, nestling beside the Wye and shielded by the formidable Black Mountains escarpment, with Hay Bluff at 2200' the foremost summit. Hay-on-Wye has many delightful features historic castles, ancient church, narrow streets, attractive buildings, but perhaps of greatest appeal to readers of this guide, the largest selection of second-hand bookshops in Britain.

The site of a Roman fort exists on the Radnorshire side of the Wye, but the real origins of the settlement stem from the construction of a Norman motte and bailey castle and a church built in the 12th century. Nearly 100 years later a larger castle was established which suffered a succession of burnings, re-buildings, attacks and capitulations by English and Welsh, including Llewelyn the Great in 1231 and Owain Glyndwr in 1400. Glyndwr survived many rebellions which continued until 1410. From then on his life, and eventually death, remain a mystery, although it is traditionally believed he was buried at Monnington, in Hereford shire, around 1416. Since the last fire of 1977 Hay Castle is in the process of being restored yet again. Its remaining smoke blackened features still dominate this small market town.

Little remains of the medieval town walls with three gates and a postern which once encircled the town, a stretch of the Wye Valley Walk hugs the course of the old wall from Black Lion Green to Newport Street. Lying outside the town walls is the parish church of St Mary's, re-built and enlarged in 1834. Its unkempt graveyard full of weathered tombs under ancient yews, surround the church.

To wander along Lion Street is to take a step back in time. The Black Lion, reputed to date from the 13th century, a former blacksmith's shop now occupied by a book-binder the accoutrements of whos trade are viewed through a window. A row of cottages, Chancery Court and Half Moon Cottage create a charming scene befor reaching Broad Street with its raised pavements. From the 19th century clock tower a selection of intriguing narrow streets and alleys lead to the castle, the colonnaded Butter Market of 1833, or past bookshops, where a vast stock is bought, sold and stored.

To the visitor it seems that every shop specialises in some aspect of the printed word. Every day of the year, except Christmas, books are swopped or sold. There are books on bees, languages, poetry, coal-mining, art, transport, archaeology and horror, together with children's books, first editions, magazines, local guides, rare bibles, photographs, prints and maps. Regular book auctions are held and one shop will find you any title you care to name. Browsers are welcome everywhere. Single items or entire libraries are disposed of and sent all round the world, and there is even a man who will measure your book space to house that prize collection of ethnography!

In 1989 the Hay Festival of Literature was born and was an immediate success. This annual event attracts first class writers to this Welsh border town.

The growth of religious dissension is evidenced by the many 18th century chapels. Evangelists, Baptists and Quakers. However, Roman Catholicism did not flourish until a congregation was established in 1926 leading to the formation of a Catholic church in 1968. Hay had its share of charities to help clothe and house the poor: there is an attractive row of 19th century almshouses on the Brecon Road.

Hay-on-Wye is an excellent centre for walkers with easy access onto the scenic ridges of the Black Mountains and the hidden valleys of the Olchon, and Honddu, Grwyne Fawr and Fechan. The Wye Valley Walk and Offa's Dyke Path both traverse the town, and the Brecon Beacons offer the energetic rambler a challenging and rewarding opportunity to explore higher peak, but care must be taken in planning your route and notice taken of weather conditions. Staff and volunteers from the Brecon Beacon National Park leads a programme of guided walks throughout the year.

There are a number of shorter family ambles around the town, Bailey Walk starting from Hay Bridge leads along the Wye to St Mary's church where seats overlook a brook and the surviving grass mound of Hay's earliest castle. Follow the watercourse to the delightful setting of Swan Well. In former days these waters were used to cure sprains to hands and feet. On a bright January day, birds anticipating spring sang their hearts out, and a dipper in his 'waiters outfit' flitted from branch to bough at the stream's edge. Alternatively, one can follow the riverside path to the Warren, a patch of uncultivated ground, with picnic tables and benches, offering views of the river and the Wyecliff opposite.

The Bailey Walk, presented to the town in 1884 by Sir Joseph Bailey, follows the course of the former horse-drawn tramway constructed in 1818 to transport coal from the Brecon and Abergavenny Canal to Talgarth, Hay and Eardisley. One horse hauled six trams carrying mainly coal as well as some limestone. Passengers were permitted at a fare of 6d. for six miles. The tramway was superseded in 1864 by the Hereford, Hay and Brecon Railway, which operated steam trains along much the same route until 1962. The station at Hay was situated below the bridge, built in 1958, replacing a series of crossings which began with an ancient ford, probably crossed by Archbishop Baldwyn and Giraldus Cambrensis in the 12th century while preaching about the third Crusades. The first toll bridge of 1763 lasted 30 years before being swept away by the tumultuous river. It was substituted by another, which in turn gave way to a Victorian iron bridge built in 1864, which due to deterioration and reduced weight limit was replaced by the present edifice.

In earlier days, during calm river conditions, barges transporting goods reached Hay, from Hereford, Chepstow and Bristol. Cargoes were handled near Wyeford, and would have served the industries of tanning, malting, and the manufacture of woollen goods. These together with the trams, trains and barges, have all disappeared, leaving Hay-on-Way a quiet, town with plenty to offer visitors. Local inhabitants are a rich mixture, ranging from hill farmers to those seeking 'alternative life styles'.

On the Radnorshire side of Hay Bridge a boundary stone indicates 1 mile and 75 yards to Kilvert's Clyro. Beyond Hay Bridge a field path leads to Wyecliff, known as Boatside in the early 19th century; the present dwelling is obscured by a high stone wall. From the cliff-top there is a pleasant view of the Wye flowing smartly around The Warren below. Wyecliffe has been partly cleared of beech and evergreens, allowing clumps of snowdrops and aconites to show their pretty faces to the wintry sun.

From here to Llowes the river meadows are rich with bird life. Flocks of tits, field fares and finches were sighted together with a pair of goosanders. The parish of Llowes nestles below hills which overlook the Wye, offering pleasing views of the subtly tinted Black Mountains. St Meilig's Church was totally re-built in 1855 except for part of its medieval tower, it also contains a damaged 13th century font and a block of limestone carved with a Celtic cross. The cross weighs 3½ tons and standing at 7 foot 6 inches high may be a prehistoric standing stone, but is traditionally linked with St Meilig, an early christian of the 7th century who settled here. The cross stood on a hillside until the 12th century, when it was moved to the graveyard. Since 1956 it has been stored inside the church for protection. This stone, also known as Maud Walbee's Stone, according to local legend, was thrown to its original position by the giantess Maud in the 12th century, when she reputedly re-built Hay castle single handed. Maud is said to have carried stones from Glasbury quarries to Hay, but on the way one fell in her shoe, she flung it away and it landed at Llowes. Her husband, William, also figures in local legends as a giant associated with Hay and Painscastle.

Llowes Court is the headquarters and workshop of Capps and Capps, restorers of old buildings, who have recently been involved in restoration of Hay Castle, Ross church and Hereford Cathedral.

Beside Llowes church an attractive stone bridge crosses a busy brook, and the nearby 17th century Radnor Arms offers sustenance before climbing to Bryn-yr-Hydd Common when circular mounds and a fortified enclosure were examined and identified in 1913. To the north the hills rise to the Begwns where The Roundabout stands at over 1300 feet in a peaceful, remote landscape for the more adventurous to explore.

On the other side of the Begwns lies Llanbedr, where a Victorian parson, the Rev. John Price, lived in the days when society tolerated eccentrics Price, from Carmarthenshire, was an educated land-owner who took over a vacant living at Llanbedr-Painscastle in 1859. He chose to live in rags in crofts and huts in squalid conditions. He had previously invented a type of shorthand, published in 1855 and was known to Kilvert as the Solitary. Price's sermons were so poorly attended that he encouraged passing vagrants by paying them to swell the congregation. The Reverend lived as a hermit until 1895 when he was hauled before the authorities as a sick man. After being stripped and scrubbed he died and was mourned for his kindness and saintly qualities. He was buried at Llanbedr church where his modest grave is easily identified.

A detour from the Wye Valley Walk between Llowes and Glasbury follows a quiet lane past Maesllwch Castle, a castellated 19th century country house belonging to the de Winton family, and partly demolished in the 1950s. Nearby, Maes-yr-onnen chapel, one of the earliest Independent churches in Wales was founded in 1696. It is still beautifully kept with original 18th and 19th century furnishings. Fresh spring flowers adorn tables and window sills.

Glasbury village with its 18th century houses and chapel on the green, has been extended and modernised during the 1900s. Continual flooding of the Wye in the past resulted in the re-siting of it's church and bridge across the river. Trailer loads of canoes have replaced wagons full of coa and lime ferried by the former tramway, and later by the Hereford, Hay and Brecon Railway. The track is still visible, but the site of the original church is difficult to identify. It was so badly damaged during 17th century floods that it was abandoned. Local legend relates that during harvesting, a white horse was seen removing the stones and timbers from the old church. In the 1660s a new building was erected on a higher site and this in turn was re-built in the 1830s.

At Glasbury Stores a charge for launching canoes is levied. A small amount to pay for a jaunt on the Wye. The river has always been used by man for navigation, but it was not until 1662 that a serious effort was made to establish it as a commercial waterway. Later acts and schemes of 1695, 1727, 1763, 1790 and 1809 attempted to improve the navigation of the river, but it proved impossible to tame. However, this did establish free navigational rights which now enables canoeists to enjoy the freedom of the Wye from Hay to Chepstow. Between Glasbury and Hay the status of navigation is unclear, but canoeists do travel unhindered within certain set times of the day.

The river crossing at Glasbury dates from Roman times with a mention of a ferry in 1311, later replaced by a succession of timber bridges. In 1777 a stone bridge was tried, which was swept away by the forceful Wye. Further structures were built in 1795, 1850 and 1922. This last being altered to its present width in 1966. Overlooking the bridge is a handsome Georgian house, Treble Hill, the former home of James Morgan who, in the 18th century, established a successful wool sorting factory in the grounds. By 1839 the business ran into financial difficulties, and the factory was converted into cottages and subsequently demolished in 1955.

During the turnpike era an incident occurred at Glasbury toll gate in 1843, when a number of men dressed in female clothes destroyed the gate before flinging it into the river. This was one of a series of uprisings in South Wales known as the Rebecca Riots, named after a verse in the Book of Genesis, and resulting in at least one murder. It forced the government to reform road administration, and helped towards the eventual demise of the turnpike system by the 1890s.

A delightful windswept route leads from Glasbury to Broughrood following an old road through meadow susceptible to flooding, although this may be solved by a new drainage scheme. The detritus from recent floods was deposited in piles on the river's bank and caught up in hedges and gateways. Pools of water submerged the old road and, together with the remains of buildings at Pwll-y-baw, made for a surrealistic scene. Buzzards soared, dippers hopped from rock to rock on the water's edge, and green and spotted woodpeckers were busy in the woodland. Flocks of sharp-eyed jackdaws soared and once rare Bewick swans, and goosanders, not sighted on the Wye before 1975, put in an appearance. Mallards were plentiful, and it is estimated that about 2,000 winter along this stretch. Smaller birds, siskin, chaffinch, blue tit and redstart were also conspicuous.

Between Boughrood and Llyswen the Wye makes an 'S', where these villages are linked by an attractive 1830s stone bridge, built by the de Wintons of Maesllwch Castle. Opposite a former toll house is the Boat Inn, a reminder that a ferry once plied the river, and on the other bank is another pub, the Bridge End Inn. From the Old Rectory at Broughrood a short detour can be followed to explore the village. A tarmac lane passes Boughrood

Castle, an early 19th century mansion, built near the site of the original Norman edifice with a stone tower recorded in 1205. Only a detached tump remains beside Castle Farm. The lane leads onto the church with its missing spire, and memorials of the de Wintons, patrons of this living in Victorian times.

At Llyswen the church with its white washed walls and organ gallery offers a modest interior, with a font dating back to an earlier Norman building. At the centuries old Griffin Inn interesting food, good wine and a huge log fire can be enjoyed before heading north along a delightful stretch to Erwood.

An eleven foot high, prehistoric standing stone is visible from the path before reaching a small sheltered graveyard enclosed by a stock-proof fence. Here lies the remains of John Macnamara of Llangoed Castle who died in 1818. By some dubious gambling debt he acquired the property with 2,500 acres around 1800. It is said the Regency rake is still seen madly driving his coach and four over the hills to the Black Mountains where he kept a mistress. From the riverside path one cannot miss the castle, now called Llangoed Hall. It was erected on an ancient site and re-built in 1632, 1802, and restored and redesigned by Clough William-Ellis during the First World War. It had fallen into decay by the 1970s but has been extensively renovated and converted into a luxurious country house hotel.

The new owners of Trericket are tastefully restoring their red bricked former corn mill are planning to offer refreshments and accommodation. The building dating from the early 18th century was driven by a water wheel until 1923, when a turbine was installed and used until the 1940s.

Trericket Mill, Erwood.

Opposite the disused mill the waymarked route re-crosses the Wye at Llanstephan over a narrow iron suspension bridge constructed in 1922. From here unmarked paths lead steeply up to the scenically sited church of St Stephen. A wonderfully peaceful and secluded graveyard is entered by an unusual 18th century lych gate with provision alongside for stabling the parson's horse.

From Llanstephan bridge a dismantled stretch of the former Mid Wales Railway has been adopted as a road, and its attractive verges have been designated as a wayside nature reserve. The road crosses a deep sided brook over a bridge dating from the railway of the 1860s. It led from the junction at Three Cocks through the Wye Valley to Builth Wells and Rhayader. This road, like the former railway, leads to the station at Erwood. This is now a craft centre where refreshments may be obtained at certain times of the year.

Erwood village lies on the western bank of the Wye, and its inn claims that Henry Mayhew stayed here when fleeing his London debtors. In the peace and tranquillity of the Wye Valley he wrote comic pieces which eventually led to the founding of Punch magazine in 1841. More recently, two movies were filmed hereabouts. For one minor scene in an American 'Werewolf in London' Crickadarn was transformed. A cottage was converted into a cosy inn, for which visitors still search, and a telephone box was disguised as a blasted oak.

Ample parking, and a picnic site, at Erwood Station make a good starting point for quite a spectacular walk to Aberedw Rocks and Llewelyn's Cave. A zig-zagging road leads steeply pas a viewpoint to a fine church at Llandeilo Graban, mainly re-built in 1897. Overlooking the Wye, its ancient yews and weathered gravestones set the scene for a dramatic tale about Radnorshire's last dragon, allegedly slain here by a ploughboy. By day the creature apparently terrorised the neighbourhood, and at night slept on top of the church tower. The young lad laid a trap by placing a dummy man there. Specially made by the local blacksmith with lethal hooks and barbs all covered in clothes. The dragon attacked the dummy and wounded itself so badly it bled to death. At the end of the 19th century a local called Meredith practised as a charmer at Llandeilo Graban. It was said he had the ability to cure bleeding, toothache and other ailments, as well as a knowledge of witchcraft, which made him feared by the neighbours.

From Llandeilo Graban church, careful navigation is required to find the way across the slopes of Llandeilo Hill to a deserted farmstead at Pantau, where in 1987 an RAF lieutenant was killed in an aircrash. The cave named after Llewelyn is not easy to find, hidden as it is in a rocky outcrop below the farm and off the right-of-way. Llewelyn, the last Welsh Prince, died in 1282 only a few years after the English King Edward I had attended and paid for his wedding in 1278.

A legend relates, Llewelyn returned to his castle at Aberedw when he heard the sounds of English troops pursuing him. He planned to shod his horse back to front, and hoped to escape by leaving a false trail, but the blacksmith betrayed the Welsh hero and Llewelyn hid overnight in a cave above the castle in Aberedw Rocks. The following day he fled to Builth seeking refuge in the castle, but was turned away. He, and his small band of men, were then followed by the English up the Irfon valley, where he was killed near Cilmery, now marked with a plain stone memorial. His head was cut off and sent to Edward I who had it displayed at the Tower of London. The fight for Welsh Independence was at an end, and the Principality was finally absorbed by the enemy.

From the small dark cave, a path descends to cross the Afon Edw, which races over mossy rocks and boulders through a deep ravine. The road leads to Aberedw church where, it is claimed, Llewelyn took communion before his death. Behind a row of houses are the remains of a castle with a licence to crenellate in 1285. In the 1860s the Mid Wales Railway was constructed across the castle site, leaving scant remnants of a moat and a round tower.

Erwood could mean either 'wood by the wandering river' or 'silver wood' and was known for its important river crossing. The current structure over the Wye replaces a 19th century iron toll bridge, which in turn succeeded a ferry and ford by drovers. For many centuries, herds from Cardigan and Carmarthen were assembled at Tregaron and driven across the Cambrian hills along a remote and wild route (which can be followed today), then taken across the hills of Mynydd Eppynt to join other herds at the Drovers Arms, an old inn now sadly boarded up and out of bounds to the public due to military activity in this beautiful, once tranquil area. The animals continued along the Twmpath to wade the Wye at Erwood.

From here great, dust raising, herds of shaggy long-horned black cattle followed a way through Painscastle to Rhydspence, and proceeded towards Hereford or re-crossed the river to follow an undefined course through the Golden Valley to Gloucester. It was recorded that 30,000 Welsh Blacks were annually driven to the south east of England during the 18th century. Drovers chose, if possible, wide soft surfaced roads and by-ways to avoid paying tolls. With the advent of the railway during the mid 19th century, long distance droving gradually disappeared.

Ponies, sheep, pigs and even geese were also herded along the drove-ways. The hooves of mountain ponies were hard enough, but cattle were shod with metal plates, pigs fitted with woollen socks with leather soles, and geese were driven through hot tar sprinkled with dry chippings. At Tregaron, behind the ancient and still cosy Talbot Hotel a field was used to shoe these animals. It must have presented a noisy, colourful and fascinating spectacle.

The approach to Builth along the Wye Valley Walk follows the traces of a former road across Alltmawr hill, and along ancient lanes, sunken with the constant wear and tear of man and animals, and rain washing away loose soil and rock. This route into Builth, clearly marked on early 19th century maps, is now abandoned, but preserved as a right-of-way. Horizontal rain obscured our view along this stretch, but in good weather Alltmawr provides a panoramic hilltop viewpoint.

At Dolfach, by an isolated cottage in a splendidly remote spot, the busy Duhonw may be forded, or crossed by a footbridge. From the top of the slope a signed footpath leads through fields to the summit of Garth Hill. Here, at 900 feet, one of the finest views is savoured, Aberedw Rocks, Erwood gorge, Radnor Forest and Mynydd Eppynt with the town of Builth Wells straddling the Wye below.

Chapter 6

BUILTH WELLS *to* RHAYADER

— FACT FILE —

Distance
20 miles (32.5 km)

Map
O.S.Landranger sheet 147

Transport
On certain days a limited bus service operates between Builth Wells and Rhayader, and there is a train service to Builth Road Station from Shrewsbury and South Wales. On weekdays a regular bus service runs between Newbridge-on-Wye and Rhayader. Contact ☎ 0597 826642/3

Parking
Builth Wells and Rhayader, along the roadside at Newbridge and Llanwrthwl.

Picnic Sites
Beside the Wye at Rhayader.

Refreshments
Builth Wells, Newbridge-on-Wye and Rhayader.

Accommodation and general visitor information
Tourist Information Centres at:
Llandrindod Wells ☎ 0597 822600
and during the season at
Builth Wells ☎ 0982 553307 & Rhayader ☎ 0597 810591.

Camp Sites
Garth and Cilmery near Builth Wells, Disserth, Howey and Rhayader.

Circular Walks
The waymarked Three Bridges Walk from Builth Wells, and following signed paths from Newbridge to Disserth, and along unsigned routes from Llanwrthwl and Rhayader.

91

Rights-of-Way Officer
Powys County Council, Llandrindod Wells
☎   *0597 826583.*

Public Telephones
Builth Wells, Goytre, Newbridge-on-Wye,
Cefn-y-Maes, Llanwrthwl and Rhayader.

Public Toilets
Builth Wells, Llanwrthwl and Rhayader.

☞ ROUTE DIRECTIONS ☜

From the **Groe** car park follow the riverside path along an avenue of trees, with the towers and spires of **Builth** forming an irregular skyline.   The **Afon Irfon** is crossed via a modern suspension footbridge, bear right to rejoin the banks of the **Wye** leading through meadows to **Penddol Rocks**, lying like grey hippos basking in the river.

The **Wye** gushes over moss covered boulders and slides through silent pools on its way to **Builth**.   The path winds through mixed woodland of birch, oak and hazel and a conifer plantation, before a steep descent leads under the **Wye Bridge** carrying the railway to and from **Builth Road Station**.

The way continues beside the **Wye** for nearly 5 miles before crossing **Nant Cilfodeg**.   Firstly through further woods and below **Coed Dolrerw**, it cuts through meadows with a succession of stiles and footbridges to be crossed along a wide shallow section of the river.   Pass a farm on the left reaching a tarmac lane, keep ahead.   This is a wonderfully tranquil stretch where an idyllically sited fishing lodge commands a picturesque riverside position.

After a footbridge over a brook the way proceeds between ivy mantled oaks at **Goytre Wood**. Upstream, the river is deep and sullen, but the path traverses pleasant undulating pastures divided by catkin bearing hedges. Above, small flocks of mewing buzzards frequently soar.

A stile and footbridge lead into a strip of dark conifers, with the **River Wye** running freely again.   The narrowing ascending path offers better views before traversing the mixed wood. It descends to the left of a timber built fishing lodge to a stile leading into meadows, where the right-of-way was diverted in 1993.

From the stile follow the route as directed, bear left over a foot-bridge crossing **Nant Cilfodeg**. Then go right across meadows to a farm at **Porthillwyd**, entering the gate beside a modern barn. Cross the farmyard and bear left across a field to a stile leading into a spinney then, within a few paces, a tarmac lane. Turn left, passing the entrance to **Trederwen**, after about 500 yards turn right across a signed stile.

The clearly marked route leads in a northerly direction through sheep pastures. Cross the swift **Hirnant**, spanned by an iron footbridge, then ascend a steep slope before continuing in the same direction across sheep filled fields to a higher spot with good views of the surrounding hills.

Descend to **Estyn Wood**, enter via a stile, the path winds between trees and over planks across marshy areas. The **Wye** comes into view again before meeting the **Beulah** to **Newbridge** road. Turn right for **Newbridge** and pass **Penybont Farm**.

If refreshments or accommodation are required continue ahead over the bridge to the village. If not, turn left before the **Wye Bridge** following a tarmac lane ascending steeply past **Llysdinam Hall**. Before reaching a white-washed cottage on the left follow the course of a recently diverted footpath on the right now clearly waymarked as the **Wye Valley Walk**. From the signed stile proceed ahead across two meadows and over a pair of foot-bridges spanning **Nant Estyn-gwyn** and its tributary.

Dipper.

Keep ahead up a sloping pasture to another stile, and continue in the same direction hugging righthand hedges through fields and over stiles until reaching a stone cottage at Ty'n-y-coed. Turn left along a track and after about 100 yards turn right over a stile and along an enclosed track leading into open fields offering excellent views of the upper Wye Valley.

Plank bridges ease the way across marshy ground, and a further succession of stiles lead through sheep pastures scattered with gnarled oak trees. A prominent signpost indicates that the Wye Valley Walk bears right over a steep sided brook by means of steps and a footbridge. Cross the stile ahead and follow the right-hand fence to reach a bend in a tarmac lane at Upper Cefncoed.

The lane meanders past the entrance to a farm at Cefncoed, then zig-zags down to cross a handsome 19th century stone bridge. From here the delightful green lane ahead leads into a perfect scene of bracken clad hills, forestry plantations, remote farmsteads and the glistening Wye below. There are other tempting paths but keep ahead past springs issuing crystal clear water from moss covered rocks.

A gap between forestry plantations provides an uninterrupted view of Doldowlod House, an attractive 19th century mansion built for James Watt, inventor of the steam engine. The property nestles beside the Wye below hills topped by the Rhiw Gwraidd TV Station. In front of the house is the disused track of the former Mid Wales Railway which once carried passengers along an attractive route between Builth and Rhayader.

The path soon descends to a gate, regretfully the open hillside path gives way to a tarmac lane on the left. Pass restored stone and timber dwellings at Hodrid. A pretty lane is followed for another mile passing Glanrhygrech, rejoining the Wye at a fishing beat known as Craig Llyn before reaching a chapel, church and, surprisingly in this little village, public toilets at Llanrwthwl.

Beside Llanwrthwl Church bear left along the Elan Village road passing a former school, then bear right up a track strewn with stone boulders, leading to restored buildings at Dolgai. A shorter and less hilly route to Glyn can be followed along the lane to the right, however,the official way is left then right to follow a bridle-way up a stony track across a bare hillside grazed by cattle and sheep.

From a gateway there is a splendid view of the patchwork of fertile fields and woods with the Wye overlooked by an undulating range of hills to the west, and **Gwastedyn Hill** with its **Jubilee Pillar** to the east. A deserted hill-farm at **Cefn** seems to encapsulate the remoteness of this windswept land-scape. A notice informs us that **Corngafallt** is a R.S.P.B. Reserve.

Further on fork right as indicated by a signpost pass an occupied farm at **Pen-y-rhiw**, where **Rhayader** and the **Afon Elan** will be sighted before descending a grassy track close to a conifer plant-ation on the left. A gate leads onto an enclosed stony track to join a tarmac lane, follow this to the right for a few hundred yards.

Turn left along a bridle-way to cross the suspension bridge over the Elan at **Glyn**: a beautiful place, hard to leave on a sunny day. On the opposite bank bear right, follow a track through **Glyn Farm**. Continue through railway remains above the **Wye**, turn left after a bend along a bridle-way following the remaining railway embankment before proceeding through a farmyard. Turn right along the enclosed bridle-way for the last climb to **Rhayader**. Within ½ mile take the tarmac lane ahead to the church at **Llansantfraed-Cwmdeuddwr**, beyond a right turn over the bridge leads into **Rhayader**, a busy and attractive town.

◆ THE UPPER WYE ◆

From Rhayader to Builth Wells the character of the Wye changes as it pours from its mountain home along its upper reaches. In turn, it appears still and sedate, then cascading over rocks, or spread over gravelly shallows it is joined by the lively waters of the Irfon, Ithon and Elan. They too start as infant streams tumbling over rock and boulder winding through a remote and beautiful landscape before meeting the Wye.

At Builth Wells the Wye offers excellent fishing and the Groe Park Angling Club controls one of the few salmon beats, open to visitors throughout the season from 26th January to 17th October. The biggest Salmon caught in these waters weighed thirty-eight and a half pounds. The prize for any angler is still a large healthy salmon, but it can be an expensive business as most of the best water is in private hands. Less costly but just as chal-lenging is trout fishing concentrated around the upper Wye and its tributaries. At Builth the river is regularly stocked with both rainbow and brown trout, and coarse fishing is allowed between June and March. Details of all fishing licences and permits are available from the Tourist Information Centre.

The River Wye is designated as a Special Site of Scientific Interest along its entire length, and graded highly for its water quality by the National Rivers Authority. Its busy flow and placid deep pools make it an ideal habitat for a large number of fish, resident and migratory. The inedible chub, the dace, pike and roach inhabit the river all year round, while its most famous visitor, the majestic salmon, migrates to the river to breed, meeting the eel going in the opposite direction. Life is rich and varied in this great waterway with fish, ranging from minnow and stickleback to sea lamprey, and the most recent intruder, the barbel.

Builth Wells is attractively sited beside the Wye in a picturesque vale sheltered by a spur of Mynydd Eppynt, the triangular hill of Garth, and Llanelwedd Rocks scarred with extensive and still active quarries. This countryside attracts tourists to Builth, to enjoy walking, pony trekking, cycling, fishing and golfing in beautiful surroundings. The town offers other sporting facilities, tennis, bowling and swimming, and there is an imaginative playground for young children. Culture too is provided by the Wyeside Arts Centre where films are shown, and plays, opera, ballet and concerts are regularly staged. Erected in 1877 as a public hall and market, the building was converted to its present use a hundred years later, and during 1993 was re-developed and extended.

There is a weekly livestock market, a lively affair, where locally bred Beulah Speckle Face, Welsh Mountain, Welsh Half Bred and Welsh Mule sheep are sold alongside cattle, now largely represented by Charolais, or Limousin, crossed with the more famous Hereford. Large autumn sheep sales are held across the river at the Royal Welsh Showground, which also houses an annual four day agricultural event attracting livestock from all over the United Kingdom. In 1993 the Royal National Eisteddfod of Wales, the largest folk festival in Europe, was held at this site.

No Roman remains have been discovered at Builth, but there is evidence of forts at nearby Beulah and Llandrindod Wells. Here in the parish of Llanfihangel Helygen are the exciting remains of Castell Collen fort constructed in the 1st century. The ramparts including a granary and bath house are visible in a lovely setting on the west bank of the Ithon. The course of a Roman road leads from here to The Gaer, a fort near Brecon. It crosses the Wye at Llechryd, where a bridle-way still fords the river, and is seen while following the Wye Valley Walk.

BUILTH WELLS *to* TRAFLE BROOK

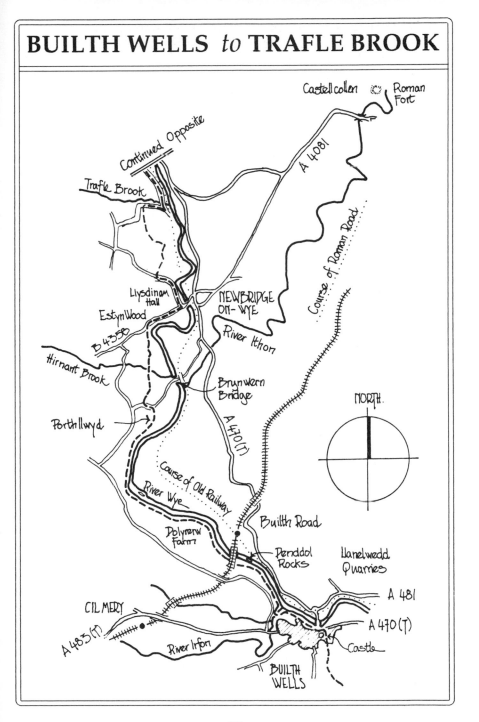

Castell collen
Roman Fort
Continued Opposite
Trafle Brook
A 4081
Course of Roman Road
Llysdinam Hall
Estyn Wood
NEWBRIDGE on-WYE
B 4358
River Ithon
Hirnant Brook
Brynwern Bridge
Porthllwyd
A 470 (T)
NORTH
Course of Old Railway
River Wye
Builth Road
Dolyrerw Farm
Penddol Rocks
Llanelwedd Quarries
CIL MERY
A 483 (T)
A 481
A 470 (T)
River Irfon
Castle
BUILTH WELLS

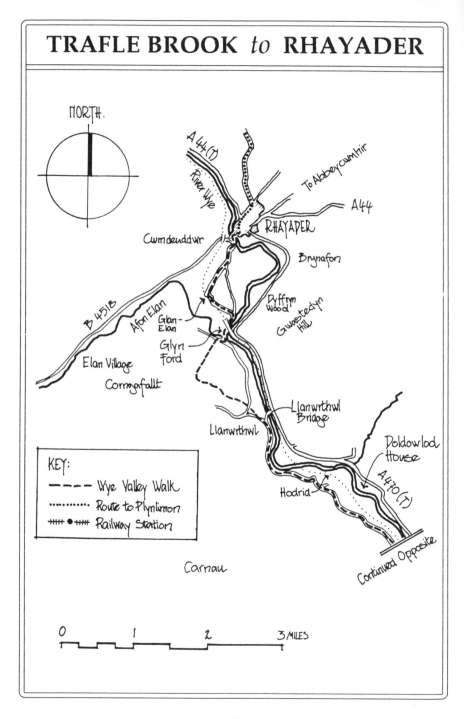

TRAFLE BROOK *to* RHAYADER

NORTH.

A 44(T)

River Wye

To Abbeycwmhir

A44

RHAYADER

Cwmdeuddwr

Brynafon

B 4518

Afon Elan

Dyffryn wood

Glan-Elan

Gwastedyn Hill

Glyn Ford

Elan Village

Corngafallt

Llanwrthwl Bridge

Llanwrthwl

Doldowlod House

A470 (T)

Hodrid

Continued Opposite

KEY:

- - - - Wye Valley Walk

.... Route to Plynlimon

+++•+++ Railway Station

Carnau

0   1   2   3 MILES

Builth developed from Norman times when a motte and bailey castle was constructed to defend an ancient river crossing. The castle was re-built during the 13th century when the parish church of St Mary's was originally erected. The new stone castle suffered further violence and intrigues, and is locally famous for setting the scene which led to the dramatic death of Llewelyn in 1282. At the end of the medieval period Builth castle fell into disuse, and was eventually demolished, its stonework plundered for other buildings in the town. What little is left of the castle is now preserved as an ancient monument, where grassy mounds remain to be investigated. A full history of this historic town site may be obtained from Builth Library.

It is almost certain that the great plague of the early 14th century reached Builth. Provisions for the inhabitants were left beside a brook called Nant yr Arian, where payment was dropped into running water to avoid risk of infection. This stream known today as the Money Brook flows into the Irfon on the outskirts of the town. It may be viewed from a bridge beside a row of cottages named after it. Over two centuries later, Builth was nearly destroyed by a fire which raged for five hours consuming forty-one dwellings. It left the place in a pitiable condition as little charitable relief was received.

Apart from its important river crossing, Builth also lies on main routes from South Wales, the North and the Midlands. In John Ogilby's Britannia of 1675 and Paterson's Itinerary of 1778 Builth is shown on the road from Chester to Cardiff. By 1822 an extended edition features Builth on the routes from London to Tregaron, Ludlow to St Davids, and Hay to Aberystwyth. The Radnorshire Turnpike Trust, formed in 1767, carried out major improvements, including an important road from Newtown to Builth connecting North and South Wales. There are references to a bridge crossing the Wye at Builth in the 13th century, certainly in 1324 a ferry was recorded here. Seventeenth century documentation reveals a timber structure, replaced by the present fine six arched stone bridge erected in 1779, and widened during the 20th century.

The north western boundaries of Builth may be investigated while exploring the Three Bridges Walk, a waymarked route of two miles starting from the Groe car park. It follows the Wye upstream until reaching the Irfon, here crossed by a modern suspension bridge built in 1984, which replaced an 1839 structure. In 1866 this was described as a picturesque but shaky affair. The route turns left past Builth Golf Club formed in 1923. The clubhouse is one of Builth's oldest buildings witha long and complicated architectural history dating from around 1550. Its cosy interior features a wonderful open fireplace and interesting timbers. The Afon Chwefri is crossed at Park Bridge, and at Pont Irfon an iron structure replaced a three span stone construction of 1787. From here a signed path descends and pleasantly follows the banks of the Irfon to return along Love Lane.

Great Spotted Woodpecker

In the 18th century mineral springs were discovered at Park Wells and in the 19th century thousands of visitors paid a few pence at a pump room to taste the saline, sulphur or chalybeate waters. This led to the building of hotels, guest houses and shops to accommodate those seeking health cures, and it was about this time that Builth added Wells to its name. It was even proposed to pipe the water to the town from Park Wells, but interest in the mineral springs declined. Today the secluded Park Wells may be approached by an unsigned path overlooking an attractive pool fed by the springs. A house and various interesting out-buildings remain in a delightful situation where a network of paths are waiting to be explored.

By the mid 1860s the railway reached this area connecting the station at Builth Road to Llandrindod, Aberystwyth, Rhayader and Hereford along the lines of the Mid Wales and the Central Wales Railways, later incorporated into the Cambrian Railway and Great Western Railway. Although many lines have closed during the 20th century, a service has survived from Builth Road to South Wales and Shrewsbury with connections to London. A date stone of 1865 is displayed on the wall of the station, now reduced both in size and status. From its platform the remnants of discontinued tracks can be seen.

On the same side as the railway station is Llanelwedd with its Victorian church beside the river. Its features include carved choir stalls, an ancient parish chest and a simple 13th century font. It is overlooked by Llanelwedd Stone Quarries, where an aggregate company produces mountains of chippings used for building and engineering works. At the turn of the century stone quarried from Llanelwedd was used to build part of the Elan Valley Waterworks .

Within a mile of Builth the Penddol Rocks are reached, an impressive and attractive feature where the Wye alternatively gushes over slippery boulders or glides silently between. During the season fishermen try their skill in the Rocks Beat which contains fishing pools named Caban, Glass, Island and Gwernyfed. Anglers have disfigured the river here by constructing concrete creels and bolted planks across natural rocks.

Upstream from Builth the riverside attracts a variety of bird life, fieldfares, nuthatches and mistle thrushes. On the water here flock of buzzards circled and soared. When we visited signs of spring were everywhere, a lone heron flapped across the sky ferrying a beak fullof sticks, robins battled for their territory and rooks cawed triumphantly in the tops of swaying evergreens. Yellow wagtails bounded and bobbed from rock to rock, and a flock of siskins filled the bushes with their cheerful chirping.

Along the river's wooded banks there were signs of badgers, those handsome pied creatures, rarely seen except at dusk. Their setts are a complicated arrangement of chambers and tunnels kept clean by their habit of digging pits outside for latrines. Otters also inhabit the banks, but are extremely shy animals who hide by day and feed at night, leaving footprints and slimy spraits as evidence of their presence. A survey carried out by the Wye Valley Countryside Service shows an encouraging increase in the population of otters occupying well established holts along the length of the Wye.

There is an exclusive stretch of fishing between Dolyrerw Farm and Porthllwyd, elegant lodges overlook tranquil beats below wooded slopes. At Porthllywd the path leads away from the river which is crossed at Brynwern by a modern bridge built in 1980 to replace an iron lattice structure erected as a toll bridge in 1885. Here above the Wye, sheep pastures are divided by hedges neatly layered, a skill essential to ,maintain their vitality and density, keeping them stockproof as well as a protection against soil erosion.

Hedgerows provide food and shelter for a great number of insects, birds and small mammals, and ancient hedges contain many rare species, including spindle, buckthorn and wayfaring. In Estyn Wood dank marshland provides an ideal site for frogs who lay their eggs in waterlogged ruts. The eggs float to the surface in a protective coat of jelly and in due course hatch into tadpoles at the end of May, developing into frogs during July, although few survive to this stage. Between the elegant pines of Estyn Wood the Wye again reveals itself. On the opposite bank at Aberithon is another boggy area, an ancient peat turbary now preserved as a nature reserve.

Seen from the Wye Valley Walk Llysdinam Hall has been the home of the Venables family since 1830 and was visited by Francis Kilvert in the 1870s. Re-built this century, the house stands near the site of a defensive ringwork constructed in Norman times to guard the river crossing. A parish church was recorded here as being in ruins at the end of the 17th century.

Over a wide part of the Wye a concrete bridge leads from Llysdinam to Newbridge-on-Wye. This 1981 bridge replaced a ferro-concrete structure opened in 1911 by Lady Venables-Llewelyn. A previous bridge dating from after the great flood of 1795 was restored in 1813 and 1853. The timbers from this may be those seen in the clear shallow waters of the river below the present structure.

Newbridge-on-Wye developed during the 19th century, and expanded with the opening of the Mid Wales Railway in 1863, although the place enjoyed an earlier history, a tribute to its importance as a river crossing. A detour around the village is recommended. From Bridge End Cottage turn right through the graveyard of the Baptist chapel, founded in 1824, and along a track to the main road under the disused railway viaduct. A milestone indicates Rhayader is eight miles distant and Builth five. Pass the New Inn, converted around 1800 from a row of 16th century cottages, with more recent additions. Opposite the pub, a drinking fountain in pink marble commemorates Newbridge's first vicar, the Rev. J.E.Lloyd, who assumed office in 1863. Follow the road towards Builth passing the Old Forge before reaching All Saints, its tower and broach spire forming a pretty picture. Return to the New Inn and turn right along the Llandrindod Road until reaching a signed footpath on the left. Keep ahead through a field and over a brook to another stile leading onto a tarmac lane. Bear left to the main road, through the village and back to the bridge.

Whilst in this area stroll across the fields from Newbridge church to Disserth. Here beside the banks of the Ithon stands a gem of church surrounded by ageing yews and weathered tombstones. A welcome notice hangs on the open door, inviting "all who are weary and desirous of rest." The white-washed building with its solid 15th century tower mercifully avoided Victorian restoration. The interior is a step back in time, wonderful boxed pews dating from the 1660s bearing the names of their former occupiers. A warm breeze from the open door gently blew dried grasses and seeds across a stone flagged floor lying below a fine timbered roof. The east walls reveal fragments of paintings and other features include a 14th century font and a 1687 three tier pulpit.

In the past horse fairs provided some excitement at Newbridge, at the annual event the streets were filled with neighing, squealing and whinnying Welsh cobs and mountain ponies of all colours, shapes and sizes. These animals were either transported by train or driven from the hills in lines of four or five tied head to tail. When mechanisation gradually replaced horse-power the fairs died out, but a livestock market survived until 1959. A reminder of this former trade was our meeting with an apprehensive colt on the road from Newbridge. He was being carefully led behind an old cream coloured pony, used as a 'school-master' to teach and train the nervous youngster.

From the bridge at Newbridge, the Wye Valley Walk now follows a recently diverted footpath instead of a network of tarmac lanes, some of which lead up to a range of hills rising to over 2,000 feet. The Trafle Brook is crossed by an attractive stone bridge built in 1839 by Thomas Price for James Watt, son of the famous inventor and steam engineer of the same name, who purchased the Doldowlod estate in the 1790s. From the walk there is a fine view of his mansion through a gap in forestry plantations. The house was built in 1827, and consists of four bays in the Elizabethan style with later additions including a tower. As Watt's son never married, the estate passed to a niece's son, provided he adopted the name Watt. The property remains with the family to this day.

Reluctantly leaving the open hillside the way from Hodrid to Llanwrthwl closely follows the Wye, where the last of the salmon beats are encountered as it is here that the water becomes more suitable for trout fishing. High redd (young trout) counts recently should result in good sport and better catches providing river levels remain suitable. Grayling numbers are on the increase, and the Rhayader area claims some of the heaviest catches with specimens weighing over 2½ pounds. Pike, chub, eel, dace and roach are plentiful, and despite a decline of our most famous fish, the Wye still remains one of the best salmon rivers in England and Wales.

Llanwrthwl is approached by a lane enclosed by mossy stone covered walls topped with harts-tongue ferns. At Mill Bridge a meandering brook nearly encircles a chapel and graveyard where tombs bear Welsh names; Jones, Evans, Powell, Williams, Price and Thomas and include both pastors and postmen. Further on an ancient stone circle leads into the churchyard of St Gwrthwyl, where a thick standing stone estimated to weigh 6 tons guards the porch. This leads into a nave and chancel of 1875, where there is an unusual four headed 11th century font, and monuments to the Clarke family from Glanrhos.

Llanwrthwl is easily accessible from Rhayader, Builth Wells and Llandrindod Wells via a wide concrete bridge over the Wye. This makes the village an ideal starting point for exploring spectacular rambles across Gwastedyn Hill, identified by its Jubilee Pillar, over Corngafallt to visit the beautiful Elan Valley, up Carnau and Drum-ddu to investigate Bronze Age burial cairns, or along the delightful Wye Valley Walk.

From Llanwrthwl a former road, known locally as Boogie Lane, steeply climbs up a pleasing boulder strewn track to Dolgai, where on the left a tumble down black granite house has been meticulously restored. A lane on the right provides an alternative route to Glyn, avoiding a demanding 1,200 foot climb to Cefn, where a deserted farm provides a prominent landmark on the bleak slopes of Corngafallt. It is here that the Royal Society for the Protection of Birds' reserve attracts skylarks, wheatear and stonechat, and where whinchat flit about in the bracken during warmer weather. Large species such as the hoarse raven with its diamond shaped tail may be seen, as well as the more familiar crow, jackdaw and rook.

The path skirts a conifer plantation with glimpses of Rhayader ahead and the Elan shimmers at the foot of the hill. Buzzards are common, and smaller, swifter birds of prey including kestrels, peregrines, sparrow-hawks and merlins might also be sighted, even the prized Welsh red kite, once widely distributed but now rare. In this virtually unspoilt area peaty hills are drained by the many streams that trickle their way down to the Wye or Elan, where damp hollows attract sedges, mosses and marsh plants.

At Glyn, the Elan flows into the Wye, where the meeting of the waters forms a tranquil spot popular with dogs and children who paddle and splash in the shallows, while their guardians snooze on sunlit banks shaded by trees. The Afon Elan may be forded, or crossed by an attractive suspension bridge, where the way proceeds on its final ascent before Rhayader. At Cwmdeuddwr a squat church dedicated to St Bride shyly stands so it is barely noticed. Re-built in 1866 by Kempson, it boasts a stained glass window by Morris & Co. Outside, the Parish Pound reflect its earlier use, and the graveyard offers a tranquil view across the Wye to Rhayader.

Chapter 7

RHAYADER to PLYNLIMON

─── FACT FILE ───

Distance
25 miles (40.5 km)

Maps
O.S. Landranger sheets 135, 136 & 147
O.S. Pathfinder sheets 928, 948 & 969

Transport
In this sparsely populated area there are only occasional buses between Rhayader, Llangurig and Pont Rhydgaled with a weekly service during the summer from Hereford to Aberystwyth. Contact Powys County Council ☎ *0597 826642/3. A Postbus serves Llangurig and surrounding areas, for further details* ☎ *0246 556728.*

Parking
Rhayader, Pont Marteg and Llangurig.

Picnic Sites
Rhayader, Pont Marteg and further afield in the Elan Valley and the Hafren Forest.

Refreshments
Rhayader, Llangurig and Pant Mawr.

Accommodation and general visitor information
Tourist Information Centres at:
Rhayader ☎ *0597 810591*
Llanidloes ☎ *0686 412605*
Aberystwyth ☎ *0970 612125.*

Camp Sites
Rhayader, Llanwrthwl & Glangwy.

Circular Walks
To the Elan Valley, and along the Radnorshire Wildlife Trust Trail at Gilfach.

106

Rights-of-Way Officer
Powys County Council, Llandrindod Wells
☎ *0597 826583.*

Public Telephones
Rhayader, Pont Marteg, Llangurig and Tyn-y-cwm.

Public Toilets
Rhayader & Llangurig.

At the time of writing the **Wye Valley Walk** ends at **Rhayader**, but requests were made to pioneer a route from here to the source of the **Wye** at **Plynlimon**.   It was a challenging task finding an acceptable way in character with the official walk, near to the banks of the river, and avoiding the busy **Aberystwyth** road. Unsigned and neglected rights-of-way were hard to find and follow, but some have been used with quiet lanes, and appropriate roads, together with an almost forgotten ford, a nature trail and a forest track.   Combined, these form our personal **Wye Valley Walk to Plynlimon**, bearing in mind that the last three miles, from the old lead mines, are across private land to the river's source. For this chapter it is advisable to use O.S. Pathfinder maps.

☞ ROUTE DIRECTIONS ☜

From **Rhayader** bridge, head initially towards the town, but take the first lane on the left to a small riverside car park. A path on the right leads along the **Wye** under an impressive mound, all that remains of **Rhayader Castle**, and into **Waun Capel Parc** with its excellent children's playground and recreational facilities. Turn right to climb a zig-zag path with the church on your left. Fork left at the top, to gain **Church Street** through an archway by the **Eagle Inn**.

Follow the road past a row of white-washed cottages and the church, re-built in 1887.   Go straight over the road junction into **Tanners Row**, which bears right to join **St Harmon Street**. Turn left, and pass a housing estate at **Maesmawr** to a lane on the left, signed to a school and a pottery. Take this lane past **Rhayader Primary School**, and the entrance to the pottery workshop, walk along a rural lane for at least another mile following an undulating route offering fine views of the **Wye Valley** to the left.

Keep straight ahead at the crossways on the crest of the hill: after about 100 yards, before the lane drops to the stone buildings at **Tynshimley,** turn left through a gate onto an enclosed track. This veers right: at a further gate, continue over the saddle of the gorse-clad hill of **Gamallt** and bear left before a steep descent to an ash coppice which shelters a stile. A grass track lined with tombstone look-alikes leads to the former farmhouse of **Gilfach,** at present being carefully and expensively converted into an Information and Accommodation Centre by the Radnorshire Wildlife Trust, where the public footpaths end. The route from here to the A470 lies within the Radnorshire Wildlife Trust's estate. Before the farm buildings cross the stile on the left, then reach a tarmac drive over another stile seen ahead. Walk down the drive to cross the **Afon Marteg** by a former railway bridge. Once over the bridge, take the stile on the left to follow the nature trail alongside the pretty gurgling, leaping, boulder strewn river. Several fields are traversed before a ladder-stile leads onto a disused railway track and bridge, re-crossing the **Afon Marteg** and continuing along the opposite bank in the same direction. Before reaching the main road, bear right over a stile, where a path leads to the road near the picnic site at **Pont Marteg.**

After a refreshment break cross the main **Rhayader** to Llangurig road, where a track ahead descends to a footbridge across the **Wye.** On the other side an indistinct right-of-way bears right, crossing sloping fields to a gate leading onto a bracken-clad slope where a sheep track winds ahead to a tarmac lane.

This tranquil gated byway is followed to the right for 2½ miles along a pleasant stretch above the **Wye,** rushing below in the rocky bottom of a wooded ravine. The river momentarily disappears and becomes visible again from the lane, which gradually ascends to a collection of buildings at **Tynant.** Take the left fork to **Pen-y-ochr,** where a public footpath bears right, through a farm, continuing along the right hand side of a verdant meadow. Midway across, the path veers slightly left then proceeds ahead through fields to a footbridge across **Nant-y-dernol.**

At this tiny hamlet turn left. Within a ¼ mile go right, through **Dernol Farm,** then immediately left following the hedge to a gate leading onto an enclosed track. Turn right along this delightful old lane lined with a colourful mixture of ferns, foxgloves, hazel, brambles and late flowering hawthorn. It bears around rejoining the lane to **Llangurig**, follow to the left past a farm at **Tan-y-birth**.

This delightful valley is enjoyed for a distance of at least three miles, passing scenic, remotely situated farmsteads, secluded cottages and swift flowing brooks, noisily cascading into the **Wye**. Within half a mile of **Llangurig** fork right and follow a straight section of road towards this last village on the **Wye**. Where its church and spire come into view a disappointing modern bridge crosses the shallow **Wye**. Ahead is **Llangurig** with everything the weary and undemanding foot-traveller may require by way of refreshment and places to stay.

On entering **Llangurig** turn left at the post office and stores and at the **Blue Bell Inn** take a right, following a lane beside a disused railway track and past the village school. Keep ahead, steeply ascending a 'No Through Road' which also serves as a right-of-way to **Bryn-y-cylla**. Bear right, around the farm buildings along an undefined footpath veering left up a hill. At the time of writing the footpath to the left from here was obstructed and reported to Powys County Council, it should descend through fields to reach a sunken way followed left to the main **Aberystwyth** road.

Turn right along the road for about ½ mile around a bend to **Bidno**. A tarmac lane on the right winds up and down to cross a shaky-looking bridge over **Nant Bidno**. Continue for another mile between bracken clad slopes and meadows dotted with grazing sheep. Beyond a small farmstead at **Glanbidno** the lane bears right but keep ahead along an overgrown track. At a derelict building fork left along a marshy bridle-path, steeply ascending the open hillside to reach the 1400 foot summit of **Pen Llwyn-leir**, to enjoy the tremendous views.

The bridle-way becomes less defined, as it winds across the summit, and heads for a gate into a young forest, replanted in 1991. Between the trees a clearer path is revealed ahead and down to a forestry road which leads onto a tarmac lane. This is followed to the left with glimpses of the **Hafren Forest** on the lower slopes of **Plynlimon**. Re-crossing **Nant Bidno** brook, the lane descends for 1½ miles between sunny banks seasonally graced with wild flowers to re-join the **Aberystwyth** road.

Turn left, along the main road for a few hundred yards, to reach a track on the right leading down to **Tyn-y-cwm**. Bear right, beyond the farm and follow the right hand hedge to a gate. From here veer

RHAYADER *to* LLANGURIG

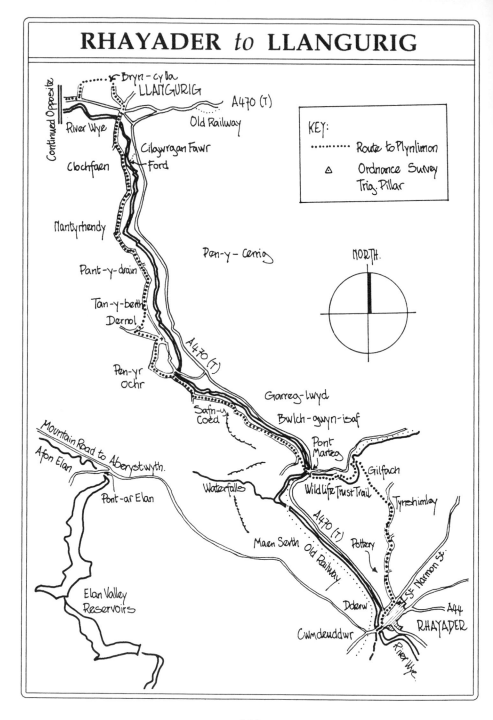

KEY:

.... Route to Plynlimon

△ Ordnance Survey Trig. Pillar

NORTH.

Bryn – cy lla
LLANGURIG
A470 (T)
Old Railway
River Wye
Cilwyrgan Fawr
Clochfaen
Ford
Continued Opposite
Nantyrhendy
Pen-y-Cerrig
Pant-y-drain
Tan-y-berth
Dernol
Pen-yr Ochr
A470 (T)
Garreg-lwyd
Safn-y-Coed
Bwlch-gwyn-isaf
Pont Marteg
Mountain Road to Aberystwyth.
Afon Elan
Gilfach
Wild Life Trust Trail
Tyrehimley
Pont-ar-Elan
Waterfalls
A470 (T)
Pottery
Maen Serth
Old Railway
St. Narmon St.
Elan Valley Reservoirs
Dderw
A44
Cwmdeuddwr
RHAYADER
River Wye

LLANGURIG *to* PLYNLIMON

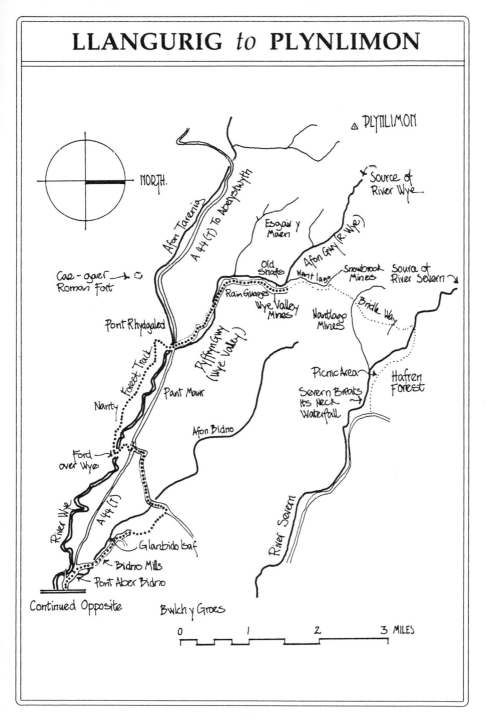

NORTH.

△ PLYNLIMON

Source of River Wye

Afon Tarenig

A44 (T) To Aberystwyth

Esgair y Maen

Afon Gwy (R. Wye)

Old Shafts

Nant Iago

Snowbrook Mines

Source of River Severn

Cae-gaer Roman Fort

Rain Guages

Wye Valley Mines

Nantlago Mines

Bridle Way

Pont Rhydgaled

Rhyfryn Gwy (Wye Valley)

Picnic Area

Hafren Forest

Forest Track

Nanty

Pant Mawr

Severn Breaks Its Neck Waterfall

Ford over Wye

Afon Bidno

River Wye

A 44 (T)

River Severn

Glanbido Isaf

Bidno Mills

Pont Aber Bidno

Continued Opposite

Bwlch y Groes

0 1 2 3 MILES

left to ford the shallows of the **Wye** across to **Hendre** where a derelict dwelling forlornly stands (if the **Wye** is not fordable, cross by a footbridge at **Nanty**).

From **Hendre** to **Nanty**, an undefined footpath above the river leads upstream through uncultivated fields and across numerous springs and bogs, all draining into the **Wye**. Traverse re-fenced fields and paddocks crossing a brook at **Nanty** where the footpath enters a farmyard. Beyond bear left into Forestry Commission plantations. The public right-of-way through the forest is difficult to find, so follow the main track ahead, running parallel to the **Wye**, for 1½ miles between thick stands of conifers. Turn right at some huts proceeding along another forest track leading to a bridge over the **Tarrenig**, flowing into the **Wye**. Cross the parking area and the main road, turn left for a few yards then right between farm buildings at **Pont Rhydgaled**. Follow the public bridle-way leading ahead towards **Plynlimon** and the **Hafren Forest**.

There is evidence that this is occasionally used as a car rally track. The youthful **Wye**, within sight as it merrily races over rocks, has to be crossed at **Pont Cefn-brwyn**. With the miniature river on the left, the path continues its ascent to disused lead mines, with old quarries, shafts and levels remaining to be investigated. Beyond a modern farm building, on the left, the river flows through this deserted valley, **Dyffryn Gwy**, from its lofty source at 2,300 feet.

This is the nearest point to the source of the **River Wye** that can be reached on a public right-of-way, from this approach. The final three miles are presently over private moorland with no acknowledged access. In any case this is rough country, where deep bogs and rocky outcrops lie in wait for the unwary, further complicated by the all too frequent hill mist. The **River Wye** rises from various non-descript springs gathering momentum, to form the stream eventually transforming into the beautiful river we now know so well, on its 155½ mile long journey to meet the **Severn** and the sea at **Chepstow**.

◆ PLYNLIMON MOUNTAINS ◆

Plynlimon, is the Anglised form of the Welsh Pumlumon, which means 'five summits'. Rising to over 2,000 feet, it forms a formidable mountain wall, within twenty miles of the Welsh coast. It is a cross-over massif, in that it is composed of Ordovician rock, common in Snowdonia, boldly outcropping here within the sleek contoured Silurian beds characteristic of mid-Wales. This wild, lonely, wind-swept transitio zone provides a challenge to even experienced walkers, for there is a lack of defined tracks across fairly rugged moorland with hidden peat bogs and rocky outcrops. A salty sea air prevails on an ascent to the source of the Wye and Severn, which rise within three miles of one another on the inhospitable slopes of Plynlimon. Both great rivers follow their individual and characteristic journeys through the Welsh border to merge again at Chepstow.

A clear day is recommended when investigating Plynlimon, for it is often hidden by swirling mists and sheets of rain. While only the sound of sheep, birds of prey and occasional low flying aircraft interrupt the silence of this bleak landscape; historically Plynlimon was the scene of violent conflict between the Welsh and English. Heroic adventures featuring Owain Glyndwr and others are re-told by travel writers, Ireland, Roscoe, Borrow, Twamley and Ritchie during the 18th and 19th centuries.

From the mid 1800s the isolated slopes of Plynlimon were scarred by unsightly lead mining, and the mountain streams were polluted by the waste from these workings. Still visible are the abandoned levels and shafts of the Wye Valley lead mines which operated between 1863 and 1885. Further north are the remains of the legendary Nantiago Silver Lead Mine situated at 1,500 feet; work started here before 1846 and despite great difficulties continued until after the First World War. Nearer to the source of the Severn early mining implements were discovered when the Snowbrook lead mine re-opened in 1860 after an estimated closure of 1,000 years. Another former mine of note, called Plynlimon, lies west of the Wye and may be approached from Eisteddfa Gurig; workings here commenced in 1866 then after a period of decline survived until 1895.

Although the slopes of Plynlimon appear barren they are in fact rich in wildlife. It is said the red grouse can be seen among patches of heather and that peregrine falcons often hover above the hills here, but neither were seen when we ascended the sinking ground to the source of the river. We did though observe an interesting range of birds, ravens gruffly chatting high up, while lower down the antics of meadow pipits, whinchats and wheatears were enjoyed. A welcome surprise in broad day-light was the large dog fox, that hopped over the infant Wye and dodged among the rocks, and a brace of hares sitting as still as a couple of brown stones. Upon being disturbed they stretched their magnificent long legs and simply galloped up the back-breaking hill.

On the banks of the Wye, Rhayader is surrounded by beautiful hills, upland plateaus and moorland divided by steep scenic valleys of the Wye, Elan, Marteg. This area attracted settlement of early man: traces of their implements, tracks, barrows, cairns, prehistoric circles and leaning standing stones are still found on the majestic hills. Maen Serth, is an ancient monolith, which was engraved as a memorial to a 12th century Welsh Prince, Einion Clud, who was murdered nearby. To reach this monument by foot from Rhayader follow the old coach road from Dderw. A continuation of this road leads to the site of a Roman marching station, though it is not easy to identify.

Red Kite.

In 1899 a priceless collection of Roman and Celtic jewels was accidently discovered by one James Marston whilst hunting foxes in the rocks of Cerrig-gwnion. With a bar he dislodged a boulder covering this valuable treasure later identified as a ring, necklet and armlet made of gold and precious stones, now thought to have belonged to the 5th century Saxon Rowena. Marston received no reward and the jewels were eventually handed to the British Museum.

From the 5th century Irish Celts travelled the countryside around Rhayader, preaching Christianity and founding 'llanau', religious enclosures. The word persists in many Welsh and border country place-names. The earliest monastic settlers followed ancient trade routes, such as the re-named The Monks Trod linking the 12th century houses at Strata Florida and Abbeycwmhir founded by the Cistercians who were granted extensive tracts of land by Rhys ap Gruffydd in 1184, known as Lord Rhys. Gruffydd wrested this bit of Wales from Norman control and in 1177 built Rhayader Castle to defend his territory.

The fragmentary remains of the Castle are approached from Castle Road leading between rows of cottages to a grassy mound topped with seats and a flag staff. Although burnt it was re-built and survived until the 14th century. Much later the ditch was filled with rubbish, and a local school-mistress cultivated the bare castle site producing a fine garden full of trees, flowers and vegetables.

North of Rhayader Castle was the Black Well, the towns main water supply which remained until the 19th century. Other springs and wells are recorded in the town, including St Mary's Well which was frequented by young couples, who for some reason, drank the spring water sweetened with sugar. A trickling spout can still be seen in Gasworks Lane. Rhayader's children were once renowned for their beauty due, it is said, from drinking Bwgey water, from the channel of spring water which at one time flowed through the town.

St Clement's Church, thought to be founded by Rhys ap Gruffydd is situated bear the castle However, the present church built in 1887 replaces that of 1772. Whilst preparing the site for a new tower in 1783, three rows of skeletons were discovered: believed to be the remains of a garrison killed by Llewelyn the Great when he destroyed the castle in the 13th century. Chapels of all denominations are a reminder of the town's nonconformity dating from the 17th century when Quakers held annual meetings in Rhayader.

The market hall, dated 1762, was demolished in 1923 and replaced by a clock tower erected by Lloyd whose descendants still work in the town. The streets of Rhayader radiate from the clock tower like compass points: West Street leads to the Wye spanned by a bridge erected in 1929, which replaced the 1780 stone arched structure. Ogilby's 1675 map indicates a wooden bridge on the Great Road from London to Aberystwyth.

The town acquired its name from a fierce cataract of water, which made a dreadful noise before the boulders that caused it were partly destroyed by explosives during the construction of the first stone bridge. The river now rushes into deep and dangerous pools now preserved as a conservation area. The occasional fat pampered trout swims lazily from here and is triumphantly caught by local lads further downstream, where Water Lane descends to a former fording place.

From the riverside car park a footpath leads below the castle mound and along the banks of the sudsy Wye, where even experienced canoeists have difficulty negotiating this fast stretch of water. Across the river are the derelict buildings of a former corn mill driven by the Nant Gwynllyn. The path continues to Waun Capel Parc which boasts tennis courts, a bowling green, football pitches and a delightful children's playground opened in 1992. This was financed by the European Development Fund as was the Leisure Centre in North Street where squash, badminton, table tennis and snooker are played. The town also offers facilities for those wishing to explore the countryside by foot, bike or pony. There cannot be many towns of similar size so blessed.

Rhayader has a range of quaint pubs including the Lamb and Flag, Cornhill, Castle, Black Lion and Royal Oak, but the timber framed Swan of 1683 with its crooked chimneys has long closed its doors to the public. It is believed some inns were established during the Tudor period to house the judge and his followers when attending the Shire Court at Rhayader. However, after a disastrous event in the 16th century, when a visiting judge was waylaid and shot, the county court was henceforth held at Presteigne and New Radnor. Inns flourished again from the late 18th century when the roads were improved by the Radnor shire Turnpike Trust which led to an increase in trade and prosperity.

Nineteenth century maps show Rhayader virtually surrounded by turnpike gates sited to collect the maximum amount of tolls for the Radnorshire Trustees. Many fine milestones remain along the highways, and former toll houses can still be recognised in South and North Streets. The unpopularity of the turnpike system in the 1840s led to the famous Rebecca Riots. In and around Rhayader men dressed as women caused havoc by continuously destroying gates and toll houses. This forced a government inquiry in 1844 leading to the formation of County Road Boards who introduced a fairer table of payments.

In the past Rhayader's industries were connected with cloth, timber, bark, wool and dairy produce. Three tan-yards were recorded including the Rhaeadr Tannery' which operated from the 18th century to the 1950s. It was re-erected in 1968 at the Welsh Folk Museum, where the unpleasant, lengthy and complicated process of tanning hides can be investigated. Tanners Row and Tan House Bridge together with a display of leather goods in Rhayader Museum are reminders of this important industry.

The small museum run by volunteers is housed in the upper storey of Bank House, built in 1881. Amongst the exhibits are a collection of gruesome and illegal poaching implements used for catching salmon and trout, memorabilia of the Mid Wales Railway which operated between 1862 and 1963, leather trade tolls, a display of boots, shoes and harness, and an interesting assortment of jars and bottles. The museum also features the history of the Elan Valley Waterworks, constructed at the turn of the 20th century. Since then Rhayader has become the focal point for touring this spectacular landscape of dams an reservoirs surrounded by rugged hills, wooded slopes and sheepwalks. Birmingham Corporation completed the project in 1904 to supply the industrial city's growing demand for water. In building these dams and reservoirs, valleys were flooded, cottagers submerged, rivers diverted, roads and railways constructed and houses built at Elan Village, with a Visitor Centre added recently. The water is conveyedto its destination through a seventy-three mile long aqueduct, together with a water supply from the remote Claerwen, dammed in 1952.

Although the previously wild and remote Elan Valley is now a popular and accessible place, a visit from Rhayader should not be missed before tackling the last stretch to the source of the Wye. A lane is followed from Rhayader towards St Harmon ascending gently under a canopy of oak, ash, beech, hazel and yew with sunlit banks of bright green ferns, deep purple foxgloves, pink tinted dog roses and a colourful blend of clover, vetch, sorrel and dried grasses. Through gateways pastoral buttercup dotted meadows grazed by ponies and sheep against a backdrop of rolling hills disappearing into the distance are constantly savoured. Further on, an ancient stone hammer was discovered at Llidiart-carnau, where a now abandoned road was used during the early 19th century for driving cattle destined for England along a route which avoided the paying of tolls. At Gamallt house platforms can be identified, probably dating from the medieval period.

Afon Marteg tumbles down from St Harmon before entering the Wye at Pont Marteg, where an attractive picnic site has been constructed by the Radnorshire Wildlife Trust. It lies within their splendid Gilfach Reserve extending to over 400 acres. The derelict farm is being converted into an information centre with accommodation. A nature trail from the farm to Pont Marteg allows ramblers and naturalists a wonderful opportunity to wander along the Marteg and absorb the beauty of the valley.

A disused railway tunnel, together with crumbling lime kilns, derelict mines and barns throughout the Wye Valley provide an ideal roost for bats. Of the fourteen species in Britain, the minute pipistrelle which could fit snugly into a match-box, is our commonest, the noctule the largest. Bats can be seen at dusk looping the loop or even landing on walls and telegraph poles as they pursue their suppers. Even the tiny pipistrelle can swallow up to 3,000 small insects a night.

At Pont Marteg a footbridge crosses the Wye and a field path joins a gated road to Llangurig. The river dances below over boulders through a delightful stretch sheltered by the rocky hills of Gerreglwyd, Bryntitley and Foel Gurig on the east and Cerrig Llwdion and Esgair Dernol on the west. Valley pastures are grazed by cows, sheep and ponies, and at Safn-y-coed an assortment of geese, hens and guinea fowl scratch and peck surrounded by fields of wild iris and buttercups bordered with forget-me-not, campion and herb robert.

Llangurig, the last village on the Wye, is approached by a modern bridge from the old road. A crossing has certainly stood here since the 18th century when it was repaired in 1713 at a cost of £20. The village lies at the junction of main routes from Aberystwyth, Rhayader and Llanidloes, with an intended train link to the Mid Wales Railway. Two pubs, a guest house, Welsh Craft Centre and post office and stores offer a welcome break for visitors, and walkers who are now within striking distance of the Plynlimon Mountains.

Around Llangurig there are a number of ancient cairns and earthworks. These include the scanty and overgrown remains of a 12th century castle at Rhyd-yr-onen, visible from a sharp bend on the road to Llanidloes. There is also the site of Cae Gaer, a Roman fort, in the middle of forestry plantations above Afon Tarrenig, a tributary of the Wye. Bwlch-y-Groes was probably named after a medieval cross which stood where ancient track converge on the desolate moors above Llangurig.

The parish church was built on the site of a Celtic monastery founded by St Currig in the 6th century. It was controlled by the Cistercians from Strata Florida during the 12th century, and portions of its massive tower date from this period. The building stands within a circular raised churchyard near the banks of the at this point shallow Wye. Coins from the reign of Henry I were discovered in a grave during the 18th century, and although documented at the time their whereabouts were unknown in 1911. St Currig's was restored in 1877 by Gilbert Scott and Baker. Some original features were preserved including a medieval nave, 15th century chancel arch, and an 18th century lych-gate with the addition of a spire, chancel arcade and stained glass windows financed by Chevalier Lloyd, a well-known local character.

Lloyd lived an interesting, religious life, and devoted his time to historical research. He inherited the estate at nearby Clochfaen. In 1885 the red marble monument outside Llangurig church was erected in his honour two years before he died. Opposite this obelisk is a drinking fountain restored in 1898 by members of the same family. There is a hint of the Arts and Crafts Movement in the fountain's lettering and in the tile hung Black Lion Inn. Other noticeable buildings in the village are Church House, dated 1896, the red brick Methodist Chapel of 1814, Smithy Cottage and the Blue Bell Inn.

Lying north of Llangurig is a secluded stretch of water known as Marsh's Pool, reflecting the grey blue tints of summer skies when we visited. It is surrounded by sloping land grazed by sheep and ponies, where a wind-swept stand of conifers and a bobbing boat on the water added to this unusual mid Welsh scene. The pool is named after T.E.Marsh, one of Llanidloes most controversial citizens in the 19th century. Another place to locate, is the almost forgotten Quakers Garden. Here an iron gate leads into a walled burial ground established in 1708, although marked with a plaque this simple graveyard is overgrown with foxgloves, holly and ash saplings.

From Llangurig a variety of unsigned paths and winding lanes lead in a north westerly direction towards the slopes of Plynlimon, where a wealth of fascinating and beautiful places may be explored and investigated. Hafren Forest with its picnic site, 'Cascades Trail' and waymarked route to the source of the Severn, while Llyn Clywedog is a picturesque reservoir where the water authority has laid out a 'Scenic Trail' with a walk through a gorge to view the preserved remains of Bryntail lead mines. From here Glyndwr's Way, a long distance walk of 120 miles, and the 274 mile long *Cambrian Way* may be joined.

From Llangurig to Pont Rhydgaled the narrowing Wye meanders through an isolated valley running hand in hand with the main Aberystwyth road. Both follow a course between tree clad slopes and bare ridges passing the remnants of a lead mine at Nanty and the Glansevern Inn at Pont Mawr. On the west bank of the stony bottomed river pleasant tracks divide impenetrable conifer plantations managed by the Forestry Commission.

The last road bridge crosses the Wye at Pont Rhydgaled, where a defined bridle-way closely follows a leaping and splashing young river rushing from the distant bleak hills. This watershed of streams, bubbling springs and oozing bogs of Plynlimon is inhabited only by sheep, whose meat is deliciously sweet, no doubt flavoured by the natural herbage of these hills. Steeper slopes are clothed with a variety of mosses, sedges and grasses while above the tiny, energetic Wye tumbles over miniature waterfalls as it swiftly flees its cradle.

❖ BIBLIOGRAPHY ❖

Barber,W.T.   Exploring Wales, *David & Charles 1982*
Barrett, Frank.   The Lady of the Flower Patch,
                               Flower Patch Publishing 1988
Bick, David.   The Old Metal Mines of Mid Wales,
                               The Pound House 1993
Black's Guide to South Wales,   *A.& C.Black 1889*
Booth, R.   Rhayader Guide, *Booth 1981*
Borrow, George.   Wild Wales, *Collins 1862*
Bradley, A.G.   Herefordshire,
                               Cambridge University Press 1913
Builth Wells Official Guide,   *B.W.O.G.Committee 1992*
Byng, Hon. John   The Torrington Dairies, 1781-94
                               re-printed Eyre & Spottiswood,

Chepstow Town Trail   *Chepstow Society 1988*
Clark, Ronald.   Bertrand Russell,
                               Thames & Hudson 1981
Clew, K.R.   Bredwardine, *Clew 1981*
Clew, K.R.   Clifford, *Clew 1982*
Clew, K.R.   Kilvert's Bredwardine, *Entwistle 1980*
Clew, K.R.   Painscastle, *Clew 1981*
Coates, S.D.   Water Mills of the Middle Wye Valley,
& Tucker, D.G   *Monmouth Museum 1983*
Collins, William   Historical Landmarks of Hereford,
                               Jakeman & Carver 1915
Coxe, Archdeacon.   An Historical Tour of Monmouthshire,
                               Coxe 1801
Cross, Bob.   Old Industrial Sites in Wyedean,
                               A.G.Cross 1982

Darby, Michael.   John Pollard Seddon,
                               Victoria & Albert Museum 1983
Davies,E.T.   Inns & Friendly Societies of Monmouth,
& Kissack,K.   *Monmouth Hist. & Educ. Trust 1981*
Davis, Hunter.   William Wordsworth,
                               Weidenfeld & Nicolson 1980
Domino   Animal Tracks & Signs, nd, *Domino*
Dreghorn, William   Geology in the Forest of Dean,
                               David & Charles 1968

Duncumbe.   General View of the Agriculture of
                             Herefordshire, *McMillan 1805*

Eagle, Dorothy &   The Oxford Literary Guide,
Carnell, Hilary   *Oxford University Press 1977*
Elan Valley Early History, nd   *U.W.I.S.T.*
Elan Valley Prehistoric, nd   *U.W.I.S.T.*
Elan Valley Roads & Ways, nd   *U.W.I.S.T.*

Fair, Geoffrey.   A History of the Hay, *Phillimore 1972*
Fitzgerald, Michael   Ancient Monuments of Wales,
                                Abercastle 1978
Forestry Commission.   Dean Forest & The Wye Valley,
                                H.M.S.O.1974
Forestry Commission.   Hafren Forest, *F.C. 1986*
Forestry Commission.   Interesting Trees of the Forest of Dean,
                             nd *F.C.*
Forestry Commission.   Walks in Tintern Woods, *F.C. 1988*
Fosbroke, Rev.T.D.   The Wye Tour, *Fosbroke 1841*
Fownhope Parish Church,   nd *Church Guide*

Gange, Edmund F.   Fownhope, *Gange 1950*
Gilbert, H.A.   The Tale of a Wye Fisherman,
                                Cape 1953
Gilpen, Rev.William   Observation on the River Wye,
                                Blamire 1789
Greer, Alfred.   Ross & the Wye Valley, *Greer c.1930*

Handley, Brian.   Wye Valley Railway,
                                Oakwood Press1982
Haslam, R.   The Buildings of Powys, *Penguin 1979*
Hay-on-Wye.   Guide & Brief History, nd
                                Hay-on-Wye T.I.C.
Hay-on-Wye.   The Bailey Walk, nd
                                Mid Wales Development
Heath, Charles.   Excursion Down the Wye, *Heath 1828*
Helme, Andrew.   Monmouth & the River Wye,
                                Alan Sutton 1989
Hereford City Guide, nd   *Hereford City Council*
Hereford Nature Trust,   Guide to Nature Reserves,
                                Hereford Nature Trust 1990
Hereford Directories,   *Cassey, Littlebury, Jakeman & Carver*
                                1857, 1867, 1902

Howes, W.H.   Disserth, *Howse 1952*
Howes, W.H.   Radnorshire, *Thurston 1949*
Hughes, Phillip.   Wales & the Drovers, *Foyles 1943*
Hurley, Heather.   The Old Roads of South Herefordshire,
                           The Pound House 1992
Hurley, Heather & Jon. Family Walks in the Wye Valley,
                           Scarthin Books 1989
Hurley, Heather & Jon. Paths & Pubs of the Wye Valley,
                           Thornhill Press 1990
Hurley Heather & Jon. Rambles & Refreshments on the Welsh
                           Borders, *Thornhill Press 1988*
Hurley, Heather.   History of the River Crossing at Wilton
                           -on-Wye, *Ross Civic Society 1993*
Hurley, Heather & Jon. Ross-on-Wye Walkabout,
                           Ross Civic Society 1990
Hutton, J.A.   Wye Salmon, *Sherratt 1949*

Ireland, Samuel.   Picturesque Views on the River Wye,
                           Faulder 1797

Jancey, Meryl, edited. St Thomas Cantilupe,
                           Friends Hereford Cathedral 1982
Jenkins, Gareth.   Blakemore's Folly,
                           Monmouth Arch Society 1975
Jenkins, Gareth.   The Rev. John Price,
                           Monmouth Arch. Society 1975
Jenkins, J.G.   The Rhaeadr Tannery,
                           Welsh Folk Museum 1973
Jervoise, E   Ancient Bridges of Wales & Western
                           England, *EP Publishing 1976*
Jones, J.G.   The History of Wales,
                           University of Wales 1990
Jones, T.   A History of Brecknock,
                           Blissett, Davies & Co revised 1911

Kissack, Keith.   Monmouth, *Phillimore 1975*
Kissack, Keith.   The River Wye, *Dalton 1978*
Kissack, Keith.   Victorian Monmouth, nd
                           Monmouth Hist. & Educ. Trust
Kissack, Keith.   A Walk Around Monmouth, nd
                           Monmouth Hist. & Educ. Trust

Lambin, D.   Foxley, *The Prices' Estate 1987*

Llangurig Parish Church, nd   *Church Guide*
Llanidloes,   *Town Guide 1988*
Look at Hereford Cathedral,   *Hereford Cathedral 1985*
Lower Wye Valley Miscellany, *Lower Wye Valley Preservation*
                             Society 1977

Maisels, F.G.   The Wildlife of the Elan & Claerwen
                     Valleys, nd *U.W.I.S.T.*
Morgan, Rev.W.   Hay & Neighbourhood, *Morgan 1932*
Morris, Martin   Book of Ross-on-Wye, *Barracuda 1980*
Morris, Martin   Reflections of Ross-on-Wye, *Morris 1973*

National Rivers Authority   Where to Fish on the Wye,
                     N.R.A. 1990

O'Donnell, Jean.   Hereford Early History,
                     Hereford City Council 1989
O'Donnell, Jean.   High Town, *Hereford City Council 1989*
O'Donnell, Jean   Norman Hereford,
                     Hereford City Council 1989
Ogilby, J.   Britannia, *Ogilby 1675*
Oppitz, L.   Hereford & Worcester Railways,
                     Countryside Books 1990
O'Shea, B. & Green, J,   In Search of Birds in Mid Wales,
                     Artery Publishing 1991

Palmer, Roy.   The Folklore of Hereford & Worcester,
                     Logaston 1992
Parr, H.W.   An Industrial Tour of the Wye Valley,
                     West London I.A.S. 1980
Patterson, Daniel   Roads, 1778, *Indust. Arch. Soc. Patterson*
                     1822, Mogg
Perks, J.C.   Chepstow Castle, *H.M.S.O. 1967*
Perman, E.P.   By-roads in South Wales,
                     Western Mail 1933
Pesvner, N.   The Buildings of Herefordshire,
                     Penguin 1963

Ramblers' Association.   Highmeadow Woods *R.A.*
Reid, Peter.   Burke & Savill's Guide to County Houses,
                     Burke's 1980
Rees, W.   An Historical Atlas of Wales, *Rees 1951*
Ritchie, L.   The Wye, *Longman 1841*

River Wye Project, Handbook, *N.R.A. 1991*

Robinson, Rev.C.   Castles of Herefordshire, *Longman 1873*

Robinson, Rev.C.   Manors & Mansions of Herefordshire,
                                    Longman 1872

Robinson, David. Tintern Abbey,
                                Welsh Historic Monuments 1986

Royal Commission on Historical Monuments.
                            Herefordshire, *H.M.S.O.1931*

Royal Commission on Historical Monuments.
                            Montgomeryshire, *H.M.S.O. 1911*

Royal Commission on Historical Monuments.
                            Radnorshire, *H.M.S.O.1913*

Salter, Mike   The Castles of Mid Wales, *Folly 1991*

Salter, Mike   The Old Parish Churches of Mid Wales,
                                    Folly 1991

Shoesmith, Ron   Alfred Watkins, *Logaston 1990*

Shoesmith, Ron   Walk Around the Medieval Defences
                     of Hereford, *Hereford City Council 1988*

Simpson, J.   The Folklore of the Welsh Borders,
                                  Batsford 1976

Skelton, S.   The Vineyards of England, *Skelton 1989*

Slater, F.M.   Newbridge-on-Wye, *Univ. of Wales 1990*

Stanford, S.C.   Archaeology of the Welsh Marches,
                                  Collins 1980

Stone, Moira.   Mid Wales Companion, *Nelson 1980*

Symonds Yat Official Guide, *Milberg 1987*

Terson, Peter.   Down the Wye, *unpublished mss 1992*

Turner, J.H.   Herefordshire Countryside Treasures,
                                  H.& W.C.C. 1981

Victoria County History of Herefordshire, *Constable 1908*

Wales Tourist Board.   The Great Nature Trail of Wales,
                            Welsh Tourist Board 1981

Ward Lock.   The Wye Valley, *Ward Lock 1914, 1960*

Waters, Ivor.   Chepstow Road Bridge,
                                Moss Rose Press 1977

Waters, Ivor.   Leather & Oak Bark at Chepstow,
                                Chepstow Society 1970

Waters, Ivor.	Piercefield, *Comber 1975*
Waters, Ivor.	Turnpike Roads, *Moss Rose Press 1985*
Waters, Ivor.	The Wine Trade of the Port of Chepstow, nd *Chepstow Society*
Wathem, J.	Wye Excursion, 1788 *unpublished mss (Hereford Record Office)*
Whitehead, David	The Principal Walk at Hereford, *Hereford Civic Society 1981*
William, J.	History of Radnorshire, *Davies 1905*
Womens' Institute.	Herefordshire Village Book, *Countryside Books 1989*
Wraight, I. & Dyer, M.	Real Ale & Cider in Herefordshire, *CAMRA 1985*
Wright, Sid.	The Birth of the Wye, *Jakeman 1946*
Wright, Sid.	Up the Claerwen, *Cornish Brothers 1948*
Wye Valley Journal,	*Wye Valley Countryside Service 1987*
Wyedean Tourist Board.	Personalities & Worthies, nd *Wyedean Tourist Board*

─────── OTHER SOURCES CONSULTED ───────

Bryants' Map of Herefordshire, 1835
Hereford County Life Magazine
Hereford Times
Ordnance Survey, Landranger sheets
Ordnance Survey, Pathfinder sheets
Ordnance Survey, Reprints of the First Edition 1 inch series.
Ross-on-Wye Civic Society Newsletters
Salmon Fishers' Maps, 1961
Transactions of the *Woolhope Naturalists' Field Club*
Correspondence from *Paul Symington* and *William Warre*, 1992

— Index —